Big Book of Beautiful Afghans™

General Information

Many of the products used in this pattern book can be purchased from local craft, fabric and variety stores, or from the Annie's Attic Needlecraft Catalog (see Customer Service information on page 71).

Contents

2 Baby Baubles

4 Berry Patch Afghan

6 Blue Cables

8 Bobbles & Squares Delight

10 Butterscotch & Caramel

12 Chevron Shells Afghan

14 Crayon Blocks Afghan

16 Desert Sky Afghan

18 Diamond Daze

20 Diamond Strip

22 Double Cable Afghan

24 Fields of Corn

26 Floral Parade

30 Formal Gardens Afghan

32 Heartstrings Afghan

34 Flower Cart

37 Irish Rose

40 Lacy Shells

42 Lavender Lace

44 Mile-a-Minute Strip Afghan

46 Purrfectly Pretty Afghan

48 Sapphire Shadows

51 Seashells Afghan

54 Shells in the Round Afghan

57 Star Dreamer

60 Southwest Ripple Afghan

62 Textured Aran Afghan

64 Wavy Shells

66 Pretty Popcorns Afghan

69 Lacy Delights

72 Stitch Guide

Baby Baubles

DESIGN BY **KATHERINE ENG**

SKILL LEVEL

INTERMEDIATE

FINISHED SIZE
30½ x 44½ inches

MATERIALS
- Bulky (chunky) weight fuzzy yarn: 29 oz/870 yds/822g white
- Size H/8/5mm crochet hook or size needed to obtain gauge
- Tapestry needle

5 BULKY

GAUGE
Rnds 1 and 2 of Square = 3 inches across
Square = 7 inches across

PATTERN NOTES
Chain-3 at beginning of row or round counts as first double crochet unless otherwise stated.

Join with slip stitch as indicated unless otherwise stated.

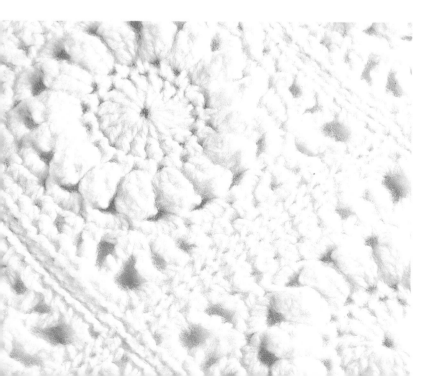

SPECIAL STITCHES
Beginning popcorn (beg pc): Ch 3, 3 dc in place indicated, drop lp from hook, insert hook in top of ch-3, pull dropped lp through.

Popcorn (pc): 4 dc in place indicated, drop lp from hook, insert hook in top of ch-3, pull dropped lp through.

INSTRUCTIONS
AFGHAN
SQUARE
MAKE 24.
Rnd 1: Ch 4, sl st in first ch to form ring, **ch 3** (see Pattern Notes), 15 dc in ring, **join** (see Pattern Notes) in 3rd ch of beg ch-3. (16 dc)

Rnd 2: Ch 1, sc in first st, ch 1, [sc in next st, ch 1] around, join in beg sc. (16 ch-1 sps)

Rnd 3: Sl st in next ch sp, **beg pc** (see Special Stitches), ch 3, [**pc** (see Special Stitches) in next ch sp, ch 3] around, join in top of beg pc.

Rnd 4: Sl st in next ch sp, ch 1, 3 sc in same sp, [ch 1, 3 sc in next ch sp] around, join with sc in beg sc. (48 sc, 16 ch-1 sps)

Rnd 5: Ch 7, **fptr** (see Stitch Guide) around joining sc, *ch 1, sk next st, dc in next st, ch 1, sk next st, hdc in next ch sp, ch 1, sk next st, sc in next st, ch 1, sk next st, sc in next ch sp, ch 1, sk next st, sc in next st, ch 1, sk next st, hdc in next ch sp, ch 1, sk next st, dc in next st, ch 1, sk next st**, (tr, ch 3, tr) in next ch sp, rep from * around, ending last rep at **, join in 4th ch of beg ch-7.

Rnd 6: Sl st in next ch-3 sp, ch 1, (2 sc, ch 3, 2 sc) in same ch sp, ch 1, [sc in next ch-1 sp, ch 1] 8 times, *(2 sc, ch 3, 2 sc) in next ch-3 sp, ch 1, [sc in next ch-1 sp, ch 1] 8 times, rep from * around, join in beg sc. Fasten off. (48 sc, 36 ch-1 sps, 4 ch-3 sps)

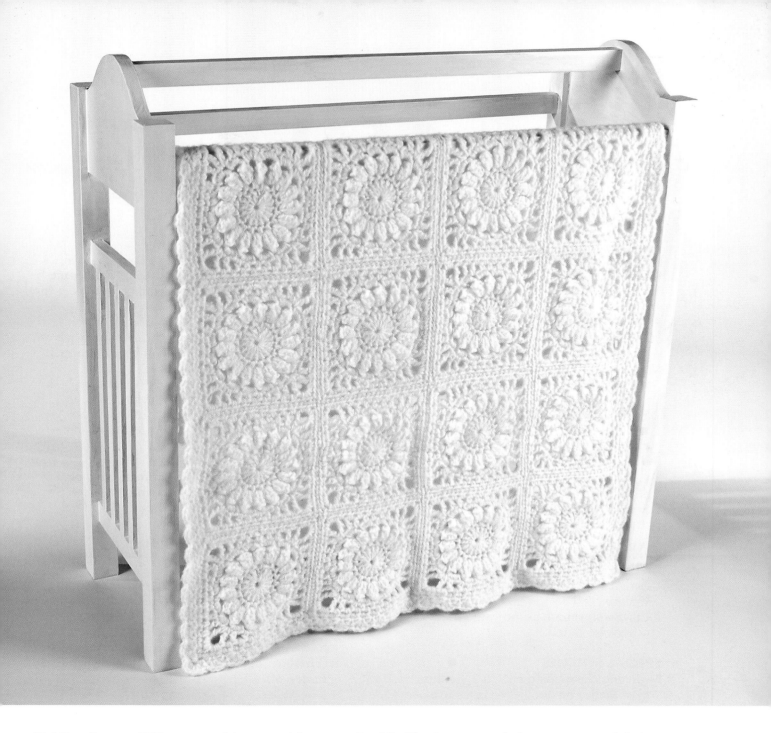

Holding Squares WS tog, matching sts, with white, sew tog through **back lps** *(see Stitch Guide)* in 4 rows of 6 Squares each.

BORDER
Rnd 1: Now working in rnds around entire outer edge, join with sc in any corner ch-3 sp, ch 3, sc in same ch sp, sc in each st, sc in each ch-1 sp, sc in each ch sp on each side of seams and sc in each seam around with (sc, ch 3, sc) in each corner ch-3 sp, join in beg sc, **turn**. *(95 sc across each short end between corner ch-3 sps, 143 sc across each long edge between corner ch-3 sps)*

Rnd 2: Sl st in next st, ch 1, sc in same st, *ch 1, sk next st, [sc in next st, ch 1, sk next st] across to next corner ch-3 sp, (sc, ch 3, sc) in next corner ch-3 sp, rep from * around, join in beg sc, turn. *(49 sc across each short end between corner ch-3 sps, 73 sc across each long edge between corner ch-3 sps)*

Rnd 3: Ch 3, 2 dc in same st, sc in next sc, 5 dc in next corner ch-3 sp, sc in next sc, *[3 dc in next sc, sc in next sc] across** to next corner ch-3 sp, 5 dc in next corner ch-3 sp, sc in next sc, rep from * around, ending last rep at **, join in 3rd ch of beg ch-3. Fasten off. ∎

Berry Patch Afghan

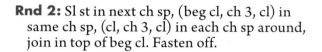

DESIGN BY **MARGRET WILLSON**

SKILL LEVEL

INTERMEDIATE

FINISHED SIZE
50 x 62 inches

MATERIALS
- Medium (worsted) weight yarn:
  25 oz/1,250 yds/709g blue
  18 oz/900 yds/510g variegated
  10 oz/500 yds/283g plum
- Size H/8/5mm crochet hook
  or size needed to obtain gauge
- Tapestry needle

MEDIUM

GAUGE
Large motif = 6 inches across

PATTERN NOTES
Chain-3 at the beginning of row or round counts
as first double crochet unless otherwise stated.

Join with slip stitch as indicated unless
otherwise stated.

SPECIAL STITCHES
Beginning cluster (beg cl): Ch 3, holding back last
lp of each st on hook, 2 dc in same place, yo,
pull through all lps on hook.

Cluster (cl): Holding back last lp of each st on
hook, 3 dc in place indicated, yo, pull through
all lps on hook.

INSTRUCTIONS
AFGHAN
LARGE MOTIF
MAKE 80.
Rnd 1: With variegated, ch 6, sl st in first ch to
form ring, **beg cl** (*see Special Stitches*) in ring,
ch 3, [**cl** (*see Special Stitches*), ch 3] 7 times,
join (*see Pattern Notes*) in top of beg cl. (*8 cls*)

Rnd 2: Sl st in next ch sp, (beg cl, ch 3, cl) in
same ch sp, (cl, ch 3, cl) in each ch sp around,
join in top of beg cl. Fasten off.

Rnd 3: Join blue in any ch sp, ch 3, (2 dc, ch 1,
3 dc) in same ch sp, (3 dc, ch 1, 3 dc) in each
ch sp around, join in 3rd ch of beg ch-3.

Rnd 4: Ch 3, (3 dc, ch 1, 3 dc) in next ch sp, *sk
next 2 sts, dc in each of next 2 sts, (3 dc, ch 1, 3
dc) in next ch sp, rep from * around to last 3 sts,
sk next 2 sts, dc in last st, join in 3rd ch of beg
ch-3. Fasten off.

With blue, sew **back lps** (*see Stitch Guide*) of
Large Motifs tog as shown in photo.

SMALL MOTIF
MAKE 63.
Rnd 1: With plum, ch 4, sl st in first ch to form
ring, ch 3, 2 dc in ring, ch 3, [3 dc in ring, ch 1]
3 times, join 3rd ch of beg ch-3. (*12 dc*)

Rnd 2: Sl st in next st, ch 3, dc in same st, (3 dc,
ch 1, 3 dc) in next ch sp, *sk next st, 2 dc in
next st, sk next st, (3 dc, ch 1, 3 dc) in next st,
rep from * around, join in 3rd ch of beg ch-3.
Fasten off.

With blue, sew back lps of Small Motifs in
openings between Large Motifs as shown
in photo.

EDGING
Rnd 1: Join plum with sc in any st, sc in each st
around with 3 sc in each corner ch sp, join in
beg sc. Fasten off.

Rnd 2: Join variegated in any center corner st,
ch 2 (*counts as first hdc*), hdc in same st, hdc
in each st around with 2 hdc in each center
corner st, join in 2nd ch of beg ch-2.
Fasten off. ■

Blue Cables

DESIGN BY **TAMMY HILDEBRAND**

SKILL LEVEL

BEGINNER

FINISHED SIZE

45 x 65 inches, excluding Fringe

MATERIALS

- Lion Brand Homespun bulky (chunky) weight yarn (6 oz/ 185 yds/170g per skein):
    7 skeins #300 hepplewhite
    5 skeins each #321 Williamsburg
    and #302 colonial
- Size N/15/10mm crochet hook or size needed to obtain gauge

GAUGE

2 dc = 1 inch; 3 pattern rows = 2 inches

PATTERN NOTE

Work with 2 strands of yarn held together unless otherwise stated.

INSTRUCTIONS
AFGHAN

Row 1 (RS): With **2 strands** (see Pattern Note) of hepplewhite held tog, ch 89, dc in 4th ch from hook, dc in next ch, [ch 1, sk next ch, dc in each of next 3 chs] 21 times, **do not turn**. Fasten off.

Row 2 (RS): Holding 1 strand each Williamsburg and colonial tog, join with sc in first st, ch 1, sk next st, sc in next st, working over ch-1 in sk chs, [tr in next sk ch, sc in next st on this row, ch 1, sk next st, sc in next st] 21 times, do not turn. Fasten off.

Row 3 (RS): Join 2 strands of hepplewhite with sc in first st, working over ch-1 in sk sts, dc in next sk st, sc in next st on this row, [ch 1, sk next st, sc in next st, dc in next sk st, sc in next st] 21 times, do not turn. Fasten off.

Row 4 (RS): Holding 1 strand of each Williamsburg and colonial tog, join with sc in first st, ch 1, sk next st, sc in next st, [**fptr** (see Stitch Guide) around next tr directly below, sc in next st, ch 1, sk next st, sc in next st] 21 times, do not turn. Fasten off.

Next rows: Rep rows 3 and 4 alternately until Afghan measures 65 inches.

Last row (RS): Join 2 strands of hepplewhite with sc in first st, working over ch-1 in sk sts, dc in next sk st, [sc in each of next 3 sts, dc in next sk st] 21 times. Fasten off.

FRINGE

Cut 1 strand of each Williamsburg and colonial, each 12 inches long. Holding both strands tog, fold in half, insert hook in st, pull fold through, pull ends through fold. Pull to secure.

Attach Fringe in each st on each short side of Afghan.

Trim all ends evenly. ■

Bobbles & Squares Delight

DESIGN BY **ELEANOR MILES-BRADLEY**

SKILL LEVEL
INTERMEDIATE

FINISHED SIZE
45 x 65 inches

MATERIALS
- Medium (worsted) weight yarn:
  32 oz/1,600 yds/907g periwinkle
  30 oz/1,500 yds/851g variegated
- Size J/10/6mm crochet hook or size
  needed to obtain gauge
- Tapestry needle

GAUGE
3 sc = 1 inch; 4 sc rows = 1 inch

PATTERN NOTE
Join with slip stitch as indicated unless
otherwise stated.

SPECIAL STITCH
Cluster (cl): Holding back last lp of each st on
hook, 3 dc in indicated place, yo, pull through
all lps on hook, ch 1 to secure.

INSTRUCTIONS
AFGHAN
MOTIF
MAKE 24.
Rnd 1 (RS): With variegated, ch 6, sl st in first
ch to form ring, ch 3 *(counts as first dc)*, 15 dc
in ring, **join** *(see Pattern Note)* in 3rd ch of beg
ch-3. *(16 dc)*

Rnd 2 (RS): Ch 5 *(counts as first dc, ch-2)*, [dc in next
dc, ch 2] around, join in 3rd ch of beg ch-5, **turn**.

Rnd 3 (WS): *(Sc, **cl**—*see Special Stitch*, sc) in next
ch-2 sp, ch 2, rep from * around, join in beg sc.

Rnd 4 (WS): Sl st across sts to first ch-2 sp, ch 1,
sc in first ch-2 sp, ch 2, [sc in next ch-2 sp, ch 2]
around, join in beg sc, **turn**. Fasten off.

Rnd 5 (RS): Join periwinkle in any ch-2 sp, ch 1,
[3 sc in each of next 3 ch-2 sps, (sc, ch 3, sc) in
next ch-2 sp] around, join in beg sc, turn.

Rnd 6 (WS): Ch 1, sc in each sc around, with
(2 sc, ch 2, 2 sc) in each corner ch-3 sp, join
in beg sc, turn.

Rnd 7 (RS): Ch 1, sc in each sc around, with (sc,
ch 2, sc) in each corner ch-2 sp, join in beg sc.
Fasten off.

Rnd 8 (WS): Join variegated in any corner ch-2
sp, ch 1, *(sc, tr, sc) in same corner ch-2 sp, [sc
in next st, tr in next st] across to corner ch-2 sp,
rep from * around, join in beg sc. Fasten off.

Rnd 9 (RS): Join periwinkle in corner tr, ch 1,
*(sc, ch 2, sc) in same corner tr, [sc in sp on rnd
below between tr, sc in top of next tr] across to
center corner tr, rep from * around, join in beg
sc, turn.

Rnd 10 (WS): Ch 1, sc in each st around, with
(sc, ch 2, sc) in each corner ch-2 sp, join in beg
sc, turn.

Rnd 11 (RS): Rep rnd 10. Fasten off.

Rnd 12 (WS): Join variegated in any st, ch 1,
sc in each st around, with (sc, ch 2, sc) in
each corner ch-2 sp, join in beg sc.

Rnd 13 (RS): Rep rnd 10. Fasten off.

Rnd 14 (WS): With periwinkle, rep rnd 8.

Rnd 15 (RS): With variegated, rep rnd 9.

Rnd 16 (WS): Rep rnd 10. Fasten off.

Rnd 17 (RS): With periwinkle, rep rnd 10. Fasten off.

ASSEMBLY
With RS of Motifs facing, working through **back lps** (*see Stitch Guide*) only, with periwinkle sew Motifs tog.

Join Motifs in 4 strips of 6 Motifs, and then join strips tog.

BORDER
With RS facing, join periwinkle in any st on edge, ch 1, evenly sp sc around entire outer edge, working 3 sc in each corner, join in beg sc. Fasten off. ■

Butterscotch & Caramel

DESIGN BY
ELEANOR MILES-BRADLEY

SKILL LEVEL

INTERMEDIATE

FINISHED SIZE
50½ x 68 inches

MATERIALS
- Medium (worsted) weight yarn:
  25 oz/1,250 yds/709g gold
  15 oz/750 yds/425g each teal
  and rust
- Size I/9/5.5mm crochet hook
  or size needed to obtain gauge
- Tapestry needle

GAUGE
7 dc = 2 inches; 2 dc and 2 sc rows = 1¾ inches
Panel = 8¼ inches wide

PATTERN NOTES
Chain-2 at beginning of row or round
counts as first half double crochet unless
otherwise stated.

Join with slip stitch as indicated unless
otherwise stated.

SPECIAL STITCH
Long half double crochet (lng hdc): Working
over next st on last rnd, yo, insert hook in
corresponding st on rnd before last, yo, pull
up long lp, yo, pull through all lps on hook.
Sk next st behind lng hdc on this rnd.

INSTRUCTIONS
AFGHAN
PANEL
MAKE 6.
Rnd 1: With gold, ch 196, dc in 4th ch from hook
(*first 3 chs count as first dc*), dc in each ch across
to last ch, 7 dc in last ch, working on opposite

side of ch, dc in each ch across to last ch, 5 dc in
last ch, **join** (*see Pattern Notes*) in 3rd ch of beg
ch-3, turn. (*396 dc*)

Rnd 2 (RS): Ch 1, (sc, ch 2, sc) in first st, *sc in
each of next 3 sts, (sc, ch 2, sc) in next st, sc in
each of next 193 sts*, (sc, ch 2, sc) in next st,
rep between * once, join in beg sc, **do not turn**.
Fasten off. (*5 sc across each short end between
corner ch-2 sps, 195 sc across each long edge
between corner ch-2 sps*)

Rnd 3: Join teal in any st, **ch 2** (*see Pattern
Notes*), hdc in each st around with (hdc, ch 2,
hdc) in each corner ch sp, join in 2nd ch of beg
ch-2, **turn**. Fasten off. (*7 hdc across each short
end between corner ch-2 sps, 197 hdc across each
long edge between corner ch-2 sps*)

Rnd 4: Join rust with sc in any corner ch sp,
(tr, sc) in same ch sp, *tr in next st, [sc in next
st, tr in next st] across** to next corner ch sp,
(sc, tr, sc) in next ch sp, rep from * around,
ending last rep at **, join in beg sc, turn.
Fasten off.

Rnd 5: Join teal in any corner tr, ch 4, hdc in
same st, *[**lng hdc** (*see Special Stitch*), [hdc in
next st on last rnd, lng hdc] across** to next
corner tr on last rnd, (hdc, ch 2, hdc) in next tr,
rep from * around, ending last rep at **, join in
2nd ch of beg ch-4, turn. Fasten off.

Rnd 6: With gold, rep rnd 3.

Rnd 7: With rust, rep rnd 3.

Rnd 8: With teal, rep rnd 4.

Rnd 9: With rust, rep rnd 5.

Rnd 10: With gold, rep rnd 3, **do not
fasten off.**

Rnd 11: Ch 2, hdc in each st around with (hdc, ch 2, hdc) in each corner ch sp, join in 2nd ch of beg ch-2. Fasten off. *(23 hdc across each short end between corner ch-2 sps, 213 hdc across each long edge between corner ch-2 sps)*

Holding Panels RS tog, matching sts, with gold, sew long edges tog through **back bars** of sts *(see Fig. 1).*

Fig. 1
Back Bar of Half Double Crochet

EDGING

Rnd 1: With WS of work facing, join gold with sc in any corner ch sp, (tr, sc) in same ch sp, *working in sts and seams, tr in next st, [sc in next st or seam, tr in next st] across** to next corner ch sp, (sc, tr, sc) in next corner ch sp, rep from * around, ending last rep at **, join in beg sc, turn.

Rnd 2: Ch 1, sc in each st around with (sc, ch 2, sc) in each corner tr, join in beg sc. Fasten off. ■

Chevron Shells Afghan

DESIGN BY **KATHERINE ENG**

SKILL LEVEL
■■■□
INTERMEDIATE

FINISHED SIZE
39 x 53 inches, excluding Fringe

MATERIALS
- Medium (worsted) weight yarn:
  24½ oz/1,225 yds/695g
    bright blue
  10½ oz/525 yds/298g bright green
  7 oz/350 yds/198g rust
  3½ oz/175 yds/99g red
- Size F/5/4mm crochet hook or size
  needed to obtain gauge

GAUGE
2 shell patterns = 2 inches; 3 shell rows =
  1½ inches

PATTERN NOTE
Chain-3 at beginning of row or round counts as
first double crochet unless otherwise stated.

SPECIAL STITCH
Shell: (2 dc, ch 2, 2 dc) in place indicated.

INSTRUCTIONS
AFGHAN
Row 1 (RS): With blue, ch 310, dc in 4th ch from
hook (*first 3 chs count as first dc*), *sk next 2 chs,
sc in next ch, [sk next 2 chs, **shell** (*see Special
Stitch*) in next ch, sk 2 chs, sc in next ch] twice,
sk next ch, shell in next ch, sk next ch, sc in next
ch, [sk next 2 chs, shell in next ch, sk next 2 chs,
sc in next ch] twice, sk next 2 chs, 2 dc in next
ch**, sk next 4 chs, 2 dc in next ch, rep from *
across, ending last rep at **, turn, sl st in next
sc, turn. Fasten off.

Row 2: Join rust with sl st in first sc, **ch 3** (*see
Pattern Note*), dc in same sc, *[sc in ch-2 sp of
next shell, shell in next sc] twice, sk next dc,
sc in next dc, shell in next ch-2 sp, sc in next
dc, [shell in next sc, sc in ch-2 sp of next shell]
twice, 2 dc in next sc**, sk next 4 dc, 2 dc in
next sc, rep from * across, ending last rep at **,
turn, sl st in next sc, turn. Fasten off.

Row 3: With green, rep row 2.

Row 4: With blue, rep row 2, **do not fasten off.**

Row 5: Ch 3, dc in same sc, *[sc in ch-2 sp of
next shell, shell in next sc] twice, sk next dc,
sc in next dc, shell in next ch-2 sp, sc in next
dc, [shell in next sc, sc in ch-2 sp of next shell]
twice, 2 dc in next sc**, sk next 4 dc, 2 dc in
next sc, rep from * across, ending last rep at **,
turn, sl st in next sc, turn. Fasten off.

Row 6: With red, rep row 2.

Next rows: Continue pattern rows 2–6 as follows:
1 green, 2 blue, 1 rust, 1 green and 4 blue.

Next rows: Rep with 1 rust, 1 red, 1 green,
2 blue, 1 rust, 1 green, 2 blue, 1 red, 1 green,
4 blue.

Next rows: Last pattern rep, beg with rust and
work 1 final row of blue. At end of last blue row,
ch 1, turn.

BORDER
Across bottom end: Sc in end dc, ch 1, sk next
dc, sc in next sc, *[ch 1, sk next 2 dc, (sc, ch 2,
sc) in ch-2 sp of next shell, ch 1, sk next 2 dc, sc
in next sc] twice, ch 2, sk next 2 dc, (sc, ch 2, sc)
in ch-2 sp at point, ch 2, sk next 2 dc, sc in next
sc**, [ch 1, sk next 2 dc, (sc, ch 2, sc) in ch-2 sp
of next shell, ch 1, sk next 2 dc, sc in next sc]
twice, ch 1, sk next 4 dc, sc in next sc, rep from
* across, ending at ** after last rep on left side
of point, ch 1, sk next dc, (sc, ch 2, sc) in top of
end ch-3.

Across first side: *Ch 3, sk end of dc or ch-3 row, sc in end of next row, rep from * across, ending with ch 3, (sc, ch 2, sc) in end ch.

Across top end: Ch 2, sk next 2 chs, sc in next ch, [ch 1, sk next 2 chs, (sc, ch 2, sc) in next ch, ch 1, sk next 2 chs, sc in next ch] twice, ch 1, sk next 3 chs, sc in next ch, *[ch 1, sk next 2 chs, (sc, ch 2, sc) in next ch, ch 1, sk next 2 chs, sc in next ch] twice, ch 3, sk next 3 chs (over dc sts), (sc, ch 2, sc) in ch-4 sp, ch 3, sk next 3 chs, sc in next ch, [ch 1, sk next 2 chs, (sc, ch 2, sc) in next ch, ch 1, sk next 2 chs, sc in next ch] twice, ch 1, sk next 3 chs, sc in next ch, rep from *

across, ending with ch 2, sk next 2 chs, (sc, ch 2, sc) in last ch.

Across 2nd side: Rep first side, ending with ch 3, (sc, ch 2, sc) in beg dc, join with sl st in beg sc. Fasten off.

FRINGE

Cut 6 strands blue, each 16 inches long. Fold strands in half, pull fold through st at bottom of Afghan, pull ends through fold, pull to secure.

Attach Fringe at each ch at point and in between points. Trim Fringe evenly. ■

Crayon Blocks
Afghan

DESIGN BY **BRENDA LEWIS**

SKILL LEVEL
■■■□ **INTERMEDIATE**

FINISHED SIZE
42 x 54 inches

MATERIALS
- Medium (worsted) weight yarn: 24½ oz/1,225 yds/695g royal blue 7 oz/350 yds/198g each red, bright green and gold
- Size I/9/5.5mm crochet hook or size needed to obtain gauge
- Tapestry needle

GAUGE
[3 dc, ch 3] 3 times = 4 inches; 6 pattern rows = 4 inches

PATTERN NOTES
Chain-3 at beginning of row or round counts as first double crochet unless otherwise stated.

Join with slip stitch as indicated unless otherwise stated.

INSTRUCTIONS
AFGHAN
BLOCK
MAKE 23.
Rnd 1: With gold, ch 8, sl st in first ch to form ring, **ch 3** (see Pattern Notes), 2 dc in ring, [ch 3, 3 dc in ring] 3 times, ch 3, **join** (see Pattern Notes) in 3rd ch of beg ch-3. Fasten off.

Rnd 2: Join green in any ch-3 sp, ch 3, (2 dc, ch 3, 3 dc) in same ch sp, * **fptr** (see Stitch Guide) around each of next 3 dc, (3 dc, ch 3, 3 dc) in next corner ch sp, rep from * twice, fptr around each of next 3 dc, join in 3rd ch of beg ch-3. Fasten off.

Rnd 3: Join red in corner ch sp, ch 3, (2 dc, ch 3, 3 dc) in same ch sp, * **bptr** (see Stitch Guide) around each of next 3 dc, fptr around each of next 3 fptr, bptr around each of next 3 dc**, (3 dc, ch 3, 3 dc) in corner ch sp, rep from * around, ending last rep at **, join in 3rd ch of beg ch-3. Fasten off.

Rnd 4: Join blue in any corner ch sp, ch 3, (2 dc, ch 3, 3 dc) in same ch sp, *[fptr around each of next 3 dc, bptr around each of next 3 bptr] twice, fptr around each of next 3 dc**, (3 dc, ch 3, 3 dc) in corner ch-3 sp, rep from * around, ending last rep at **, join in 3rd ch of beg ch-3. Fasten off.

Sew 3 Blocks tog in a row for center.

FIRST LACY INSERTION
Rnd 1: Join blue in corner ch sp, working down long edge, ch 3, (2 dc, ch 3, 3 dc) in same ch sp, *[ch 3, sk next 3 sts, dc in each of next 3 sts] 3 times, ch 3, sk next 3 sts, dc in sp before seam, dc in seam, dc in sp after seam, rep from * across to last block, [ch 3, sk next 3 sts, dc in each of next 3 sts] 3 times, ch 3, sk next 3 sts, (3 dc, ch 3, 3 dc) in corner, [ch 3, sk next 3 sts, dc in each of next 3 sts] 3 times, ch 3, sk next 3 sts**, (3 dc, ch 3, 3 dc) in corner, rep from * to **, join in 3rd ch of beg ch-3.

Rnds 2–8: Sl st to corner ch-3 sp, ch 3, (2 dc, ch 3, 3 dc) in same ch sp, *ch 3, sk next 3 dc, 3 dc in next ch-3 sp, rep from * across to next corner sp, ch 3**, (3 dc, ch 3, 3 dc) in corner sp, rep from * around, ending last rep at **, join in 3rd ch of beg ch-3. At end of last row, fasten off.

Sew 3 Blocks tog in a row, sew to narrow end of center piece.

Rep for other end.

Sew 7 Blocks tog in a row, sew to side, making sure end Blocks of row are even with Blocks on ends of center piece. Rep for rem side.

2ND LACY INSERTION
Rnds 1–8: Rep rnds 1–8 of First Lacy Insertion.

BORDER
Rnd 1: Join gold in any corner ch sp, ch 3, (2 dc, ch 3, 3 dc) in same ch sp, *[fptr around each of next 3 dc, 3 dc in next ch-3 sp] across to last 3 dc before corner sp, fptr around each of last 3 dc**, (3 dc, ch 3, 3 dc) in corner ch sp, rep from * around, ending last rep at **, join in 3rd ch of beg ch-3. Fasten off.

Rnd 2: Join green in any corner ch sp, ch 3, (2 dc, ch 3, 3 dc) in same corner ch sp, *[bptr around each of next 3 sts, fptr around each of next 3 sts] across to last 3 dc before corner sp, bptr around each of last 3 sts**, (3 dc, ch 3, 3 dc) in corner ch sp, rep from * around, ending last rep at **, join in 3rd ch of beg ch-3. Fasten off.

Rnd 3: Join red in any corner ch sp, ch 3, (2 dc, ch 3, 3 dc) in same corner ch sp, *[fptr around each of next 3 sts, bptr around each of next 3 sts] across to last 3 dc before corner ch sp, fptr around each of last 3 sts**, (3 dc, ch 3, 3 dc) in corner ch sp, rep from * around, ending last rep at **, join in 3rd ch of beg ch-3. Fasten off. ∎

Desert Sky Afghan

DESIGN BY MAGGIE WELDON

SKILL LEVEL

BEGINNER

FINISHED SIZE
51 x 65 inches

MATERIALS
- Bulky (chunky) weight yarn:
  25 oz/875 yds/709g blue
  15 oz/525 yds/425g each
  blue variegated and white
- Size I/9/5.5mm crochet hook
  or size needed to obtain gauge
- Tapestry needle

GAUGE
Rnds 1 and 2 = 2¾ inches
Square = 6½ inches

PATTERN NOTES
Chain-3 at beginning of row or round counts as
first double crochet unless otherwise stated.

Join with slip stitch as indicated unless
otherwise stated

SPECIAL STITCH
Puff stitch (puff st): [Yo, insert hook in place
indicated, yo, pull up lp even with hook] 4
times *(9 lps on hook)*, yo, pull through 8 lps
on hook, yo, pull through all lps on hook.

INSTRUCTIONS
AFGHAN
SQUARE A
MAKE 32.
Rnd 1 (RS): With blue, ch 4, sl st in first ch to
form ring, **ch 3** *(see Pattern Notes)*, 2 dc in ring,
ch 2, [3 dc in ring, ch 2] 3 times, **join** *(see Pattern
Notes)* in 3rd ch of beg ch-3. *(12 dc)*

Rnd 2 (RS): Sl st in each of next 2 sts, sl st in next
ch-2 sp, ch 3, (2 dc, ch 2, 3 dc) in same ch sp, ch

1, [(3 dc, ch 2, 3 dc) in next ch-2 sp, ch 1] around,
join in 3rd ch of beg ch-3. Fasten off. *(24 dc)*

Rnd 3 (RS): Join white in any corner ch-2 sp, ch 1,
[sc in corner sp, ch 5, **puff st** *(see Special Stitch)*
in last sc, sc in same corner sp, ch 3, puff st in
last sc, sc in next ch-1 sp, ch 3, puff st in last sc]
4 times, join in beg sc. Fasten off. *(12 puff sts)*

Rnd 4 (RS): Join variegated in any corner ch-5
sp, ch 3, (2 dc, ch 2, 3 dc) in same ch sp, ch 1,
[3 dc in next ch-3 sp, ch 1] twice, *(3 dc, ch 2,
3 dc) in next ch-5 sp, ch 1, [3 dc in next ch-3 sp,
ch 1] twice, rep from * around, join in 3rd ch of
beg ch-3.

Rnd 5 (RS): Sl st in each of next 2 sts, sl st in next
ch-2 sp, ch 3, (2 dc, ch 2, 3 dc) in same ch sp, ch
1, [3 dc in next ch-1 sp, ch 1] 3 times, *(3 dc, ch
2, 3 dc) in next ch-2 sp, ch 1, [3 dc in next ch-1
sp, ch 1] 3 times, rep from * around, join in 3rd
ch of beg ch-3. Fasten off. *(60 dc)*

SQUARE B
MAKE 31.
Rnds 1 & 2: With variegated, rep rnds 1 and 2
of Square A.

Rnd 3: Rep rnd 3 of Square A.

Rnds 4 & 5: With blue, rep rnds 4 and 5
of Square A.

ASSEMBLY
Squares are sewn tog 7 x 9, alternating Squares
A and B. Beg and end first row of Squares
with Square A, beg and end 2nd row of Squares
with Square B, continue to rep until all Squares
are joined.

EDGING
Rnd 1 (RS): Join blue in any corner, ch 3, (2 dc,
ch 2, 3 dc) in same corner sp, ch 1, *[3 dc in
next ch-1 sp, ch 1] 4 times, ◊3 dc in joining, ch
1, [3 dc in next ch-1 sp, ch 1] 4 times, rep from

◊ across to next corner sp**, (3 dc, ch 2, 3 dc) in next corner sp, ch 1, rep from * around, ending last rep at ** join in 3rd ch of beg ch-3. Fasten off.

Rnd 2 (RS): Join white in any corner ch-2 sp, ch 1, sc in same sp, *ch 5, puff st in last sc, sc in same corner sp, ch 3, puff st in last sc, [sc in next ch-1 sp, ch 3, puff st in last sc] rep across to next corner ch-2 sp**, sc in corner ch-2 sp, rep from * around, ending last rep at **, join in beg sc. Fasten off.

Rnd 3 (RS): Join variegated in any corner ch-5 sp, ch 3, (2 dc, ch 2, 3 dc) in same corner sp, ch 1, *[3 dc in next ch-3 sp, ch 1] across edge to

next corner ch-5 sp**, (3 dc, ch 2, 3 dc) in next ch-5 sp, ch 1, rep from * around, ending last rep at **, join in 3rd ch of beg ch-3. Fasten off.

Rnd 4 (RS): Join blue in any corner ch-2 sp, ch 3, (2 dc, ch 2, 3 dc) in same corner sp, ch 1, *[3 dc in next ch-1 sp, ch 1] across to next corner ch-2 sp**, (3 dc, ch 2, 3 dc) in corner ch-2 sp, ch 1, rep from * around, ending last rep at **, join in 3rd ch of beg ch-3. Fasten off.

Rnd 5 (RS): Join white in any corner ch-2 sp, ch 1, *sc in corner ch-2 sp, [ch 4, sk next dc, puff st in next dc, sk next dc, ch 4, sc in next ch-1 sp] across edge to next corner ch-2 sp, ch 4, rep from * around, join in beg sc. Fasten off. ■

Diamond Daze

DESIGN BY **DIANE POELLOT**

SKILL LEVEL

INTERMEDIATE

FINISHED SIZE
50 x 66 inches

MATERIALS
- Medium (worsted) weight yarn:
  54 oz/2,700 yds/1,531g purple
- Size J/10/6mm crochet hook or size
  needed to obtain gauge

GAUGE
1 block = 1¼ inches square

PATTERN NOTES
Chain-3 at beginning of row or round counts as
first double crochet unless otherwise stated.

Join with slip stitch as indicated unless
otherwise stated.

SPECIAL STITCH
Block: Pull up lp in each of next 5 sts (*6 lps on
hook*), yo, pull through 1 lp on hook, [yo, pull
through 2 lps on hook] 5 times (*1 lp on hook*),
*sk first vertical bar, pull up lp in each of next
5 vertical bars, insert hook in next dc, yo, pull
though st and 1 lp on hook, [yo, pull through 2
lps on hook] 5 times, rep from * twice, sk first
vertical bar, sl st in each of next 5 vertical bars.

INSTRUCTIONS
AFGHAN
Row 1: Ch 164, 4 dc in 4th ch from hook (*first 3
chs count as first dc*), sk next 3 chs, sc in next ch,
[sk next 3 chs, 9 dc in next ch, sk next 3 chs, sc

in next ch] across to last 4 chs, sk next 3 chs,
5 dc in last ch, turn. (*201 sts*)

Row 2: Working this row in **back lps** (*see Stitch
Guide*) only, ch 1, sc in first st, [**block** (*see
Special Stitch*), sc in next dc] across, turn.

Row 3: Working this row in **front lps** (*see Stitch
Guide*) only, ch 3, **dc dec** (*see Stitch Guide*) in
next 5 sts, ch 1 for eye, [ch 3, sc in next st or
row, ch 3, dc dec in next 9 sts, ch 1 for eye]
across to last 5 sts or rows, ch 4, sc in end of
next row, ch 3, dc dec in same row and last 4
rows, ch 1 for eye, turn.

Row 4: Ch 3, 4 dc in eye of first st, [sk next ch sp,
sc in next sc, sk next ch sp, 9 dc in eye of next
st] across to last 2 sts and 2 ch sps, sc in next sc,
5 dc in eye of last st, **do not turn**. Fasten off.

Row 5: Working this row in back lps only,
join with sc in first st, [block, sc in next dc]
across, turn.

Rows 6–78: [Rep rows 3–5 consecutively]
25 times, ending last rep with row 3.

Rnd 79: Working around outer edge, rep row 4,
ending with 13 dc in last eye, working down
side of Afghan, *sc in st at corner of next
block, [9 dc in next eye, sc in st at corner of
next block] across*, working in starting ch on
opposite side of row 1, 13 dc in ch at base of
next 5-dc group, sc in ch at base of next sc, [9 dc
in ch at base of next 9-dc group, sc in ch at base
of next sc] across, 13 dc in ch at base of last 5-dc
group, working up side of Afghan, rep between
* once, 8 dc in same eye as first ch-3, join with
sl st in 3rd ch of beg ch-3. Fasten off. ■

Diamond **Strip**

DESIGN BY **MAGGIE WELDON**

SKILL LEVEL

BEGINNER

FINISHED SIZE
45 x 65 inches

MATERIALS
- Red Heart Classic medium (worsted) weight yarn (3½ oz/ 190 yds/99g per skein):
  7 skeins #853 soft navy
  5 skeins #3 off-white
  2 skeins #645 honey gold
- Size I/9/5.5mm crochet hook or size needed to obtain gauge
- Stitch marker

MEDIUM

GAUGE
6 dc = 2 inches
Diamond = 1¼ inches square
Strip = 5 inches wide

PATTERN NOTES
Chain-3 at beginning of row or round counts as first double crochet unless otherwise stated.

Join with slip stitch as indicated unless otherwise stated.

INSTRUCTIONS
AFGHAN
STRIP
MAKE 10.
CENTER DIAMONDS
Row 1: With off-white, ch 8, dc in 4th ch from hook, dc in each of next 3 chs, leaving last ch unworked, turn.

Row 2: Ch 3 (*see Pattern Notes*), dc in each of next 3 sts.

Next rows: Rep Rows 1 and 2 alternately until 24 Diamonds are completed, ending last rep with row 2, ch 1. Fasten off.

BORDER
Rnd 1: With any side facing and working across 1 side of all Diamonds, **join** (*see Pattern Notes*) navy in ch-1 at either end of Diamonds, ch 4 (*counts as first tr*), 11 tr in same ch, **sc in point of first Diamond, *7 tr in ch-1 between next 2 Diamonds, sc in next point, rep from * 22 times, 12 tr in end ch, working on opposite side, rep from **, omitting last 12 tr, join in 4th ch of beg ch-4. Fasten off. (*394 sts*)

Rnd 2 (RS): Join gold in first tr of rnd 1, ch 1, sc in same st, *[ch 1, sc in next tr] 11 times, ch 1, sk next st, [sc in next st, ch 1, sk next st] across to first tr of end 12-dc group**, rep from *, ending last rep at **, join in beg sc. Fasten off. (*208 ch-1 sps*)

Rnd 3 (RS): Join off-white in first ch-1 sp of rnd 2, ch 3, place marker in beg ch-3, dc in same ch-1 sp, 2 dc in each ch-1 sp around, join in 3rd ch of beg ch-3. Fasten off. (*416 dc*)

Rnd 4 (RS): Join navy in sp before marked ch-3 of rnd 3, ch 3, dc in same sp, [2 dc in sp between next 2-dc group] twice, [3 dc in sp between next 2-dc group] 6 times, [2 dc in sp between next 2-dc group] 100 times, [3 dc in sp between next 2-dc group] 6 times, [2 dc in sp between next 2-dc group] 97 times, join 3rd ch of beg ch-3. Fasten off. (*428 dc*)

Sew long sides of Strips tog as shown in photo. ∎

Double Cable Afghan

DESIGN BY **CAROLYN CHRISTMAS**

SKILL LEVEL

EASY

FINISHED SIZE
60 x 66½ inches

MATERIALS
- Medium (worsted) weight yarn: 40 oz/2,000 yds/1,134g plum
- Size I/9/5.5mm crochet hook or size needed to obtain gauge
- Tapestry needle

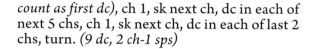

4

MEDIUM

GAUGE
Strip = 8¼ inches wide

PATTERN NOTES
Chain-3 at the beginning of row or round counts as first double crochet unless otherwise stated.

Join with slip stitch as indicated unless otherwise stated.

SPECIAL STITCHES
Beginning cluster (beg cl): Ch 3, holding back last lp of each st on hook, dc in same place, yo, pull through all lps on hook.

Cluster (cl): Holding back last lp of each st on hook, 2 dc in place indicated, yo, pull through all lps on hook.

Picot: Ch 3, sl st in 3rd ch from hook

INSTRUCTIONS
AFGHAN
STRIP
MAKE 7.
CENTER
Row 1: Ch 13, dc in 4th ch from hook (*first 3 chs count as first dc*), ch 1, sk next ch, dc in each of next 5 chs, ch 1, sk next ch, dc in each of last 2 chs, turn. (*9 dc, 2 ch-1 sps*)

Row 2: **Ch 3** (*see Pattern Notes*), dc in next st, ch 1, sk next ch sp, **bpdc** (*see Stitch Guide*) around each of next 2 sts, dc in next st, bpdc around each of next 2 sts, ch 1, sk next ch sp, dc in each of last 2 sts, turn.

Row 3: Ch 3, dc in next st, ch 1, sk next ch sp, sk next 3 sts, **fptr** (*see Stitch Guide*) around each of next 2 sts, working behind last 2 fptr, dc in 3rd sk st, working in front of last 2 fptr, fptr around each of first and 2nd sk sts, ch 1, sk next ch sp, dc in each of last 2 sts, turn.

Row 4: Rep row 2.

Row 5: Ch 3, dc in next st, ch 1, sk next ch sp, fpdc around each of next 2 sts, dc in next st, fpdc around each of next 2 sts, ch 1, sk next ch sp, dc in each of last 2 sts, turn.

Rows 6–89: [Rep rows 2–5 consecutively] 21 times. At end of last row, **do not turn or fasten off.**

EDGING
Rnd 1: Now working in rnds and in ends of rows, ch 1, sc in first row, [ch 1, sc in next row] across, ch 1, working in starting ch on opposite side of row 1, sc in first ch, ch 1, sk next ch, sc in next ch, [ch 1, sk next 2 chs, sc in next ch] twice, ch 1, sk next ch, sc in last ch, ch 1, [sc in next row, ch 1] across, sc in first st, ch 1, sk next st, sc in next ch sp, ch 1, sk next 2 sts, sc in next st, ch 1, sk next 2 sts, sc in next ch sp, ch 1, sk next st, sc in last st, ch 1, **join** (*see Pattern Notes*) in beg sc. (*188 sc, 188 ch-1 sps*)

Rnd 2: **Beg cl** (*see Special Stitches*), ch 1, [**cl** (*see Special Stitches*) in next sc, ch 1] 89 times, *sk

next ch sp, (tr, ch 1, tr) in next ch sp, ch 1, tr in next sc, (ch 1, tr in same sc) 4 times, ch 1, (tr, ch 1, tr) in next ch sp, ch 1*, [cl in next sc, ch 1] 91 times, rep between * once, cl in last sc, ch 1, join in top of beg cl. *(200 ch-1 sps)*

Rnd 3: Sl st in first ch sp, ch 1, sc in same ch sp, ch 1, [sc in next ch sp, ch 1] around, join in beg sc. Fasten off.

JOIN STRIPS
Holding 2 Strips RS tog, working through both thicknesses, join with sc in first ch sp, [ch 3, sk next ch sp, sc in next ch sp] 44 times, leaving rem sts unworked. Fasten off.

Join rem Strips in same manner.

BORDER
Rnd 1: Working around entire outer edge, join with sc in 11th ch sp before first joining seam on 1 short end, ◊*ch 1, [cl in next ch sp, ch 1] 3 times, (cl, ch 1, cl, ch 1) in each of next 3 ch sps, [cl in next ch sp, ch 1] 3 times**, sc in next ch sp, ch 1, sk next joining seam, sc in next ch sp, rep from * 6 times, ending last rep at **◊, [sc in next ch sp, ch 1] 91 times, rep between ◊ once, [sc in next ch sp, ch 1] 90 times, join in beg sc.

Rnd 2: Sl st in first ch sp, ch 1, sc in same ch sp, [ch 3, sc in next ch sp] 5 times, *◊ch 5, sk next ch sp, sc in next ch sp, [ch 3, sc in next ch sp] 4 times, ch 1, sk next 3 ch sps, sc in next ch sp, [ch 3, sc in next ch sp] 4 times, rep from * 5 times, ch 5, sk next ch sp, sc in next ch sp, [ch 3, sc in next ch sp] 5 times◊, [ch 1, sc in next ch sp] 91 times, rep between ◊ once, ch 1, [sc in next ch sp, ch 1] 90 times, join in beg sc.

Rnd 3: Sl st in first ch sp, ch 1, 3 sc in same ch sp, ◊*3 sc in each of next 3 ch sps, (hdc, 2 dc) in next ch sp, (dc, **picot**—*see Special Stitches,* 3 dc, picot, 3 dc, picot, dc) in next ch sp, (2 dc, hdc) in next ch sp**, 3 sc in each of next 3 ch sps, sk next ch sp, rep from * 6 times, ending last rep at **, 3 sc in each of next 4 ch sps, ch 1, [sc in next ch sp, ch 1] 91 times◊, 3 sc in each of next 4 ch sps, rep between ◊ once, join in beg sc. Fasten off. ∎

Fields of Corn

DESIGN BY **MELISSA LEAPMAN**

SKILL LEVEL

BEGINNER

FINISHED SIZE
46 x 56 inches

MATERIALS
- Elmore-Pisgah Peaches & Crème medium (worsted) weight cotton yarn (2½ oz/122 yds/71g per ball): 17 balls #10 yellow
- Size H/8/5mm crochet hook or size needed to obtain gauge

GAUGE
3 dc and 2 ch-1 sps = 1 inch; 3 dc pattern rows = 1¾ inches

PATTERN NOTES
Chain-4 at beginning of row or round counts as first double crochet and chain-1 unless otherwise stated.

Join with slip stitch as indicated unless otherwise stated.

SPECIAL STITCH
Shell: 5 dc in place indicated.

INSTRUCTIONS
AFGHAN
Row 1 (RS): Ch 188, dc in 6th ch from hook (*first 5 chs count as first dc, sk 1 ch and ch-1*), ch 1, sk next ch, dc in next ch, *sk next 2 chs, **shell** (*see Special Stitch*) in next ch, sk next 2 chs, [dc in next ch, ch 1, sk next ch] twice, dc in next ch, rep from * across, turn.

Row 2: Ch 4 (*see Pattern Notes*), dc in next dc, ch 1, dc in next dc, *sk next 2 dc of shell, shell in next dc of shell, sk next 2 dc of shell, [dc in next dc, ch 1] twice**, dc in next dc, rep from * across, ending last rep at **, sk next ch, dc in next ch of turning ch, turn.

Next rows: Rep row 2 until Afghan measures 55 inches from beg, ending on WS row.

Last row (RS): Ch 4, dc in next dc, ch 1, dc in next dc, *ch 2, sk next 2 dc of shell, sc in next dc, ch 2, sk next 2 dc of shell, [dc in next dc, ch 1] twice**, dc in next dc, rep from * across, ending last rep at **, sk next ch, dc in next ch of turning ch. Fasten off.

BORDER
Rnd 1 (RS): Join (*see Pattern Notes*) in any st, ch 1, evenly sp sc around entire outer edge, working 3 sc in each corner st, join in beg sc.

Rnds 2 & 3: Ch 1, sc in each sc around, working 3 sc in center sc of each corner, join in beg sc. At end of last rnd, fasten off. ■

Floral Parade

DESIGN BY **DOT DRAKE**

SKILL LEVEL
■■■□ **INTERMEDIATE**

FINISHED SIZE
54 x 76 inches

MATERIALS
- Medium (worsted) weight yarn:
  24 oz/1,200 yds/680g raspberry
  16 oz/800 yds/454g each pink,
  light celery and soft white
  8 oz/400 yds/227g lilac
- Medium (worsted) weight fleck yarn:
  12 oz/600 yds/340g celery
- Size G/6/4mm crochet hook
  or size needed to obtain gauge
- Tapestry needle

GAUGE
7 sc = 2 inches
Large Motif = 10 inches
Small Motif = 4 inches

PATTERN NOTES
Chain-3 at beginning of row or round counts as
first double crochet unless otherwise stated.

Join with slip stitch as indicated unless
otherwise stated.

INSTRUCTIONS
AFGHAN
LARGE MOTIF
MAKE 35.
*Note: Rnds 1–5 of Large Motif are worked
from outer edge to center.*

Rnd 1 (RS): With celery, ch 96, using care not to
twist ch, sl st in first ch to form ring, **ch 3** (*see
Pattern Notes*), dc in each of next 3 chs, ch 10,
[dc in each of next 4 chs, ch 10] around, **join**
(*see Pattern Notes*) in 3rd ch of beg ch-3. Fasten
off. (*96 dc, 24 ch-10 sps, 24 groups 4-dc*)

Rnd 2 (RS): Join raspberry in 2nd dc of any 4-dc
group between ch-10 sps, ch 3, dc in next dc, dc
in each of 2nd and 3rd dc of next 4-dc between
ch-10 sps, ch 10, *[dc in each of 2nd and 3rd dc
of next 4-dc group between ch-10 sps] twice,
ch 10, rep from * around, join in 3rd ch of beg
ch-3. (*48 dc, 12 ch-10 sps, 12 groups 4-dc*)

Rnd 3 (RS): Join pink in 2nd dc of any 4-dc
group between ch-10 sps, ch 3, dc in next dc,
ch 10, [dc in each of 2nd and 3rd dc of next 4-dc
group between ch-10 sps, ch 10] around, join in
3rd ch of beg ch-3. Fasten off. (*24 dc, 12 ch-10
sps, 12 groups 2-dc*)

Rnd 4: Join white in first dc, ch 3, dc in next dc,
ch 10, [dc in each of next 2 dc between ch-10
sps, ch 10] around, join in 3rd ch of beg ch-3.
Fasten off. (*24 dc, 12 ch-10 lps, 12 groups 2-dc*)

Place Motif on flat surface with rnd 1 on outside
of circle, remembering that rnd 1 has 24 ch-10
sps and all rem rnds have 12 ch-10 sps. *Insert
hook in ch sp to right on rnd 1, insert hook
in next ch sp of rnd 1 to the left, pull this lp
through first ch sp, insert hook in ch sp directly
above rnd 2, pull this lp through lp on hook,
pull lp directly above rnd 3 through lp on hook,
pull lp directly above rnd 4 through lp on hook,
remove hook. Rep from * until all lps around
Motif are chained toward center of Motif.
(*12 ch sps at center*)

Rnd 5: Working at center of Motif, with light
celery, leaving long end at beg, ch 4, sc in 1 ch
sp at center, ch 3, sl st in first ch of beg ch-4, [ch
3, sc in next ch sp at center, ch 3, sl st in same
first ch of beg ch-4] around. Leaving long end,
fasten off. Secure beg and ending ends to keep
center secure.

Rnd 6 (RS): Working in starting ch of opposite side of rnd 1, join white in any ch, sl st in each ch around.

Rnd 7: Ch 1, sc in first st, ch 3, sk next sl st, [sc in next sl st, ch 3, sk next sl st] around, join in beg sc. Fasten off.

Rnd 8: Working in back of previous rnd, join pink in first sk st, ch 1, sc in same st, *ch 5, sc in next sk sl st, rep from * 4 times, ch 7**, sc in next sk sl st, rep from * around, ending last rep at **, join in beg sc. Fasten off. *(8 ch-7 sps, 40 ch-5 sps)*

Rnd 9: Join light celery in first ch-5 sp, ch 1, beg in same ch sp, [2 sc in each of next 5 ch-5 sps, (2 sc, ch 2, 2 sc) in next ch-7 sp] around, join in beg sc. *(112 sc, 8 ch-2 sps)*

Rnd 10: Ch 1, sc in each sc around with 2 sc in each ch-2 sp, join in beg sc. Fasten off. *(128 sc, 16 sc each side edge)*

SMALL MOTIF
MAKE 32.

Rnd 1: With lilac, ch 5, 3 dc in first ch of ch-5, [ch 3, 4 dc in same first ch of beg ch-5] 3 times, ch 3, join in 5th ch of beg ch-5. Fasten off.

Rnd 2: Join white in ch-3 sp, ch 3, (3 dc, ch 5, 4 dc) in same ch-3 sp, ch 2, [(4 dc, ch 5, 4 dc) in next ch-3 sp, ch 2] around, join in 3rd ch of beg ch-3. Fasten off.

Rnd 3: Join light celery in any ch-5 sp, ch 1, [6 sc in ch-5 sp, sc in each of next 4 dc, 2 sc in next ch-2 sp, sc in each of next 4 dc] around, join in beg sc. Fasten off. *(64 sc, 16 sc each side edge)*

ASSEMBLY
Working in **back lps** *(see Stitch Guide)* only, sew Large Motifs tog 5 x 7, according to **Diagram** *(see Fig. 1)*, working across 16 sc sts of side edge.

Sew Small Motifs between Large Motifs.

BORDER
With RS facing, join raspberry in first sc of any corner 2 sc worked in ch-2 sp of rnd 10, ch 1, *sc in each of next 2 sc on point of Motif, ch 6, drop lp from hook, insert hook in previous sc, pick up dropped lp and pull through st on hook, (3 sc, ch 3, sl st in first ch of ch-3) 3 times in next ch-6 sp, 3 sc in next ch-6 sp, sc in each sc until next 2-sc group worked at point, rep from * around, working ch-6 sps over 3rd and 4th sc sts of each Small Motif, at each joining of 2 Motifs, ch 1, sk last sc of working Motif and first sc of next Motif, sc in next sc, join in beg sc. Fasten off . ∎

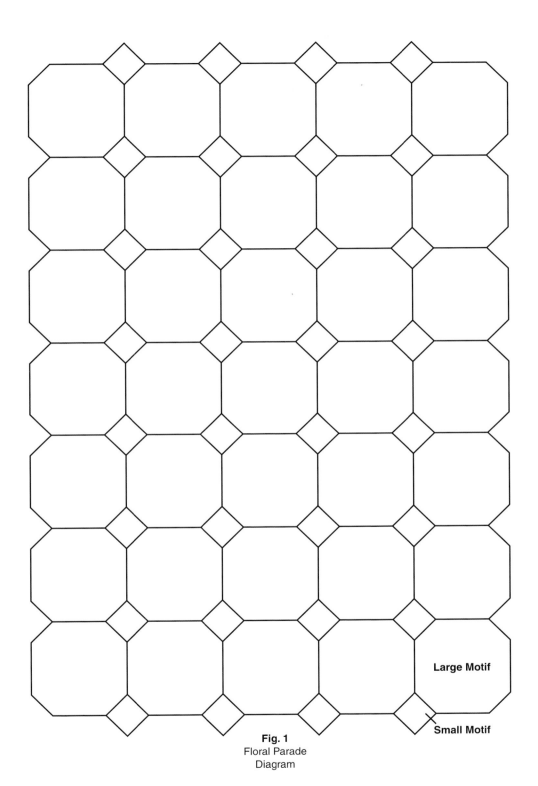

Large Motif

Small Motif

Fig. 1
Floral Parade
Diagram

Formal Gardens
Afghan

DESIGN BY **CHRISTINA MCNEESE**

SKILL LEVEL
INTERMEDIATE

FINISHED SIZE
46 x 65 inches, excluding Fringe

MATERIALS
- Medium (worsted) weight yarn: 16 oz/800 yds/454g each raspberry, green and Aran
- Size H/8/5mm crochet hook or size needed to obtain gauge

MEDIUM

GAUGE
11 sts = 4 inches; 5 dc rows = 4 inches

PATTERN NOTES
Chain-3 at the beginning of row or round counts as first double crochet unless otherwise stated.

Each square on chart equals 1 double crochet

INSTRUCTIONS
AFGHAN
Row 1: With green, ch 128, dc in 4th ch from hook (*first 3 chs count as first dc*), **changing colors** (*see Stitch Guide*) in last st worked, rep **Chart** (*see Fig. 1*) 7 times across, turn. (*126 dc*)

Rows 2–14: Ch 3, dc in each dc across, changing colors according to Chart, turn.

Rows 15–70: [Rep rows 1–14 of Chart consecutively] 4 times. At end of last row, fasten off.

FRINGE
Cut 5 strands 12 inches long, using 1 color for each Fringe, fold strands in half, pull fold through st at bottom of Afghan, pull ends through fold, pull to secure.

Evenly sp 29 Fringe across top and bottom edges of Afghan, alternating colors as shown in photo. Trim ends evenly. ■

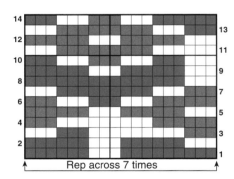

Rep across 7 times

Fig. 1
Formal Gardens Afghan
Chart

COLOR KEY
□ Aran
■ Green
■ Raspberry

Heartstrings Afghan

DESIGN BY **MARGRET WILLSON**

SKILL LEVEL
■■■□
INTERMEDIATE

FINISHED SIZE
46 x 64 inches

MATERIALS
- Medium (worsted) weight yarn:
  17 oz/850 yds/482g dark pink
  15 oz/750 yds/425g lavender ombré
  12 oz/600 yds/340g white
- Size H/8/5mm crochet hook or size needed to obtain gauge
- Tapestry needle

GAUGE
3 dc = 1 inch; 2 dc rows = 1 inch
Panel = 4½ inches wide

PATTERN NOTES
Chain-4 at the beginning of row or round counts as first double crochet and chain-1 unless otherwise stated.

Chain-3 at the beginning of row or round counts as first double crochet unless otherwise stated.

Join with slip stitch as indicated unless otherwise stated.

INSTRUCTIONS
AFGHAN
PANEL
MAKE 10.
CENTER
Row 1: Starting at bottom, with pink, ch 14, dc in 6th ch from hook (*first 5 chs count as sk 1 ch, dc and ch-1*), [ch 2, sk next 2 chs, dc in next ch] twice, ch 1, sk next ch, dc in last ch, turn. (*5 dc*)

Row 2 (RS): **Ch 4** (*see Pattern Notes*), sk next dc, 5 dc in next dc, ch 1, sk next dc, dc in last dc, turn. (*7 dc*)

Row 3: **Ch 3** (*see Pattern Notes*), 2 dc in next dc, dc in each of next 3 dc, 2 dc in next dc, dc in last dc, turn. (*9 dc*)

Row 4: Ch 4, **dc dec** (*see Stitch Guide*) in next 4 sts, ch 3, dc dec in last worked dc and next 3 dc, ch 1, dc in last dc, turn. (*4 dc*)

Row 5: Ch 4, dc in next dc, ch 2, dc in next ch-3 sp, ch 2, dc in next dc, ch 1, dc in last dc, turn. (*5 dc*)

Rows 6–93: [Rep rows 2–5 consecutively] 22 times. At end of last row, fasten off.

BORDER
Rnd 1: With bottom RS of Center facing, working around outer edge, **join** (*see Pattern Notes*) white in last ch sp, (ch 3, 2 dc, ch 3, 3 dc) in same ch sp, *2 dc in each end of next 91 rows, (3 dc, ch 3, 3 dc) in next corner, 2 dc in each of next 2 ch sps*, (3 dc, ch 3, 3 dc) in next corner, rep between * once, join in 3rd ch of beg ch-3. Fasten off. (*10 dc across each short edge, 188 dc across each long edge for a total of 396 dc, 4 corner ch sps*)

Rnd 2: Join lavender in first corner ch sp, (ch 3, 2 dc, ch 3, 3 dc) in same ch sp, *sk next dc, dc in each of next 186 dc, sk next dc, (3 dc, ch 3, 3 dc) in next corner ch sp, sk next dc, dc in each of next 8 dc, sk next dc**, (3 dc, ch 3, 3 dc) in next corner ch sp, rep from * around, ending last rep at **, join in 3rd ch of beg ch-3. Fasten off. (*14 dc across each short edge, 192 dc across each long edge for total of 412 dc*)

ASSEMBLY
Match and sew **back lps** (*see Stitch Guide*) of sts on long edges of Panels tog.

EDGING

Working around outer edge, join lavender in first corner ch sp at top of 1 short edge, ch 3, 5 dc in same ch sp, dc in each st, 2 dc in each ch sp around with 5 dc in each corner ch sp, join 3rd ch of beg ch-3. Fasten off. ∎

Flower Cart

DESIGN BY **DOT DRAKE**

SKILL LEVEL

EASY

FINISHED SIZE
60 x 62 inches

MATERIALS
- Medium (worsted) weight yarn:
  24 oz/1,200 yds/680g white
  8 oz/400 yds/227g each lilac,
  lavender, pink and raspberry
- Medium (worsted) weight fleck yarn:
  18 oz/900 yds/510g celery
- Size G/6/4mm crochet hook or
  size needed to obtain gauge

GAUGE
4 sc = 1 inch
Circular Motif = 8 inches in diameter

PATTERN NOTES
Chain-3 at beginning of round counts
as first double crochet unless
otherwise stated.

Join with slip stitch as indicated unless
otherwise stated.

INSTRUCTIONS
AFGHAN
CIRCULAR MOTIF
MAKE 30 WITH MC OF 8 EACH
OF RASPBERRY AND LILAC AND
7 EACH OF LAVENDER AND PINK.
FIRST TRIANGLE
Rnd 1: With MC, ch 5, 3 dc in 5th ch from hook,
[ch 3, 4 dc in same 5th ch from hook] twice, ch
3, **join** (see Pattern Notes) in top of beg ch-5.
Fasten off.

Rnd 2: Join white in any ch-3 sp, **ch 3** (see
Pattern Notes), (3 dc, ch 5, 4 dc) in same ch-3
sp, ch 2, [(4 dc, ch 5, 4 dc) in next ch-3 sp, ch 2]
twice, join in 3rd ch of beg ch-3. Fasten off.

Rnd 3: Join celery in any ch-5 sp, ch 1, 2 sc in
same ch-5 sp, [sc in each of next 4 dc, 2 sc in
next ch-2 sp, sc in each of next 4 dc, 6 sc in
next ch-5 sp] twice, sc in each of next 4 dc, 2 sc
in next ch-2 sp, sc in each of next 4 dc, 4 sc in
same ch-5 sp as beg 2-sc, join in beg sc. Fasten
off. (48 sc)

2ND TRIANGLE
Rnds 1–3: Rep rnds 1–3 of First Triangle, to
within joining of rnd 3. Insert hook in top lp of
first sc of working Triangle and with WS tog
into top lp of previous Triangle in 4th sc of any
6-sc corner, sl st Triangles tog across 13 sts,
leaving rem sts unworked. Fasten off.

Continue to rep 2nd Triangle, joining to previous
Triangle, joining 6th Triangle to previous and
first to close the circle.

CENTER
Join white in any sc at center of Circular Motif,
ch 1, working around center of Circular Motif,
work 2 sc in each Triangle around center, join
in beg sc. Fasten off. (12 sc)

BORDER
Working around outer edge of Circular Motif,
join white in first sc of any Triangle, ch 1, *sc
in first sc on Triangle, [ch 3, sk 1 sc, sc in next
sc] 9 times, rep from * across each of the 6
Triangles, join in beg sc. Fasten off.

Following **Diagram** (see Fig. 1 on page 36),
continue to work Border on each Circular
Motif, joining edges to previous Motifs by

working [ch 1, sc in ch-3 sp on adjacent Motif, ch 1, sk next sc on working Motif, sc in next sc] across edge to be joined to adjacent Motifs until all Motifs are joined.

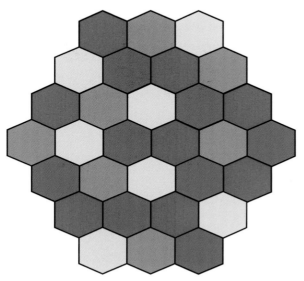

Fig. 1
Flower Cart
Diagram

COLOR KEY
- Raspberry
- Lavender
- Lilac
- Pink

TRIM

Rnd 1: Join white in 4th ch-3 sp before joining of any 2 Motifs, ch 1, sc in same ch-3 sp, *[ch 5, dc in 5th ch from hook] 3 times (*this forms 3 ch sps to span from 1 motif to the next*), sk next 6 ch sps (*3 from working motif and 3 from next*), sc in next ch sp, [ch 4, sc in next ch sp] across to 4th sp before next joining, rep from * around, ending with ch 2, dc in beg sc to position hook in center of last ch sp.

Rnd 2: Ch 1, sc in same sp as beg ch-1, [ch 4, sc in next ch sp] around, ending with ch 2, dc in beg sc.

Rnds 3 & 4: Rep rnd 2. At the end of last rnd, ch 4, join in beg sc. Fasten off.

Rnd 5: Join lilac in any ch sp, ch 1, [3 sc in next ch sp, 2 sc in next ch sp] around, join in beg sc.

Rnd 6: Ch 4, sk next sc, [dc in next sc, ch 1, sk next sc] around, join in 3rd ch of beg ch-4.

Rnd 7: Ch 1, sc in each dc and each ch-1 sp around, join in beg sc.

Rnd 8: Working in reverse direction, [ch 4, drop lp from hook, sk next sc, insert hook in next sc, pick up dropped lp and pull through st] around, join in same st as beg ch-4. Fasten off. ■

Irish Rose

DESIGN BY **ELIZABETH ANN WHITE**

SKILL LEVEL

■■□□

EASY

FINISHED SIZE

54 x 64 inches

MATERIALS

- Fine (baby) weight pompadour yarn: 50 oz/5,000 yds/1,418g white
- Size H/8/5mm crochet hook or size needed to obtain gauge

FINE

GAUGE

4 dc = 1 inch; 2 dc rows = 1 inch
Panel = 25½ x 34 inches
Motif = 8½ inches square

PATTERN NOTES

Chain-3 at beginning of row or round counts as first double crochet unless otherwise stated.

Join with slip stitch as indicated unless otherwise stated.

INSTRUCTIONS
AFGHAN
CENTER PANEL

Row 1: Ch 97, dc in 4th ch from hook (*first 3 chs count as first dc*) and in each ch across, turn. (*95 dc*)

Row 2: Ch 3 (*see Pattern Notes*), dc in each st across, turn.

Row 3: Ch 3, dc in each of next 4 sts, *ch 4, sk next 6 sts, (dc, ch 2) 3 times in next st, dc in same st, ch 4, sk next 6 sts, dc in each of next 5 sts, rep from * across, turn. (*6 dc groups, 25 ch sps*)

Row 4: Ch 3, dc in each of next 4 sts, *ch 2, sk next ch-4 sp, 5 dc in next ch-2 sp, [sc in next dc, 5 dc in next ch-2 sp] twice, ch 2, sk next ch-4 sp, dc in each of next 5 dc, rep from * across, turn. (*105 dc*)

Row 5: Ch 3, dc in each of next 4 sts, *ch 4, sk next ch-2 sp, (dc, ch 2) 3 times in center dc of next 5-dc group, dc in same dc, ch 4, sk next ch-2 sp, dc in each of next 5 dc, rep from * across, turn. (*6 dc groups, 25 ch sps*)

Rows 6–56: [Rep rows 4 and 5 alternately] 25 times, ending last rep with row 4.

Row 57: Ch 3, dc in each of next 4 sts, *ch 6, sk next 5-dc group, sc in center dc of next 5-dc group, ch 6, sk next 5-dc group, dc in each of next 5 dc, rep from * across, turn. (*6 dc groups, 10 ch sps*)

Row 58: Ch 3, dc in each dc and in each sc across with 6 dc in each ch sp, turn. (*95 dc*)

Row 59: Ch 3, dc in each st across. Fasten off.

MOTIF
MAKE 18.
Rnd 1: Ch 4, sl st in first ch to form ring, ch 4 *(counts as dc and ch-1)*, [dc in ring, ch 2] 5 times, join with sl st in 3rd ch of beg ch-4. *(6 dc, 6 ch sps)*

Rnd 2: Ch 1, (sc, ch 1, 5 dc, ch 1, sc) in each ch sp around, **join** *(see Pattern Notes)* in beg sc. *(6 petals)*

Rnd 3: Working behind petals, [ch 3, sl st in **back strands** of last sc *(see Fig. 1)* on this petal and first sc on next petal] 6 times, join in 3rd ch of beg ch-3. *(6 ch sps)*

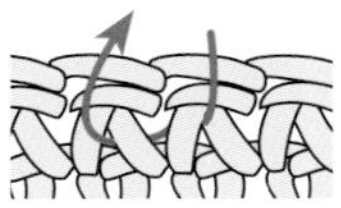

Fig. 1
Back Strands of Single Crochet

Rnd 4: Ch 1, (sc, ch 1, 7 dc, ch 1, sc) in each ch sp around, join in beg sc. *(6 petals)*

Rnd 5: Working behind petals, [ch 4, sl st in back strands of last sc on this petal and first sc on next petal] 6 times, join in first ch of beg ch-4. *(6 ch sps)*

Rnd 6: Ch 3, 7 dc in first ch sp, 8 dc in each ch sp around, join 3rd ch of beg ch-3. *(48 dc)*

Rnd 7: (Ch 4—*counts as first tr*, 2 tr, ch 2—*corner*, 3 tr) in first st, ch 3, sk next 3 sts, sc in next st, [ch 3, sk next st, sc in next st] twice, ch 3, sk next 3 sts, *(3 tr, ch 2—*corner*, 3 tr) in next st, ch 3, sk next 3 sts, sc in next st, [ch 3, sk next st, sc in next st] twice, ch 3, sk next 3 sts, rep from * around, join in 4th ch of beg ch-4. *(20 ch sps)*

Rnds 8 & 9: Sl st across to next ch sp at corner, (sl st, ch 3, 2 dc, ch 2, 3 dc) in same ch sp, ch 3, [sc in next ch sp, ch 3] across to next corner ch sp, *(3 dc, ch 2, 3 dc) in corner ch sp, ch 3, [sc in

next ch sp, ch 3] across to next corner ch sp, rep from * around, join 3rd ch of beg ch-3. *(24 ch sps, 28 ch sps)*

Rnd 10: Ch 3, dc in each dc and 3 dc in each ch-3 sp around with (2 dc, ch 2, 2 dc) in each corner ch-2 sp, join in 3rd ch of beg ch-3. *(28 dc on each side, 4 corner ch sps)*

Rnd 11: Ch 3, dc in each dc around with (2 dc, ch 2, 2 dc) in each corner ch-2 sp, join in 3rd ch of beg ch-3. Fasten off. *(32 dc on each side, 4 corner ch sps)*

ASSEMBLY
Matching sts, sl st Motifs tog through the **back lps** *(see Stitch Guide)*, forming 2 short strips, each 3 Motifs long and 2 long strips, each 6 Motifs long.

Easing to fit, sl st 1 short strip to starting ch on row 1 of Center Panel, sl st other short strip to last row of Center Panel.

On each side, easing to fit Center Panel and matching sts on Motifs, sl st 1 long strip to ends of short strips and ends of rows on Center Panel.

BORDER
Rnd 1: Join with sc in any corner ch sp, ◊ch 5, sk next 2 sts, [sc in next st, ch 5, sk next 2 sts] 10 times, *sc in next ch sp, ch 5, sc in next ch sp, ch 5, sk next 2 sts, [sc in next st, ch 5, sk next 2 sts] 10 times*, rep between * across to next corner, (sc, ch 5, sc) in corner ch sp, rep from ◊ twice, ch 5, sk next 2 sts, [sc in next st, ch 5, sk next 2 sts] 10 times, rep between * across, ch 2, join with dc in joining sc.

Rnds 2–12: Ch 1, sc in joining ch sp, (ch 5, sc) in each ch sp around with (ch 5, sc) twice in each corner ch sp, ch 2, join with dc in first sc.

Rnd 13: Ch 1, 3 sc in joining ch sp, (3 sc, ch 3, sl st in last sc made, 3 sc) in each ch-5 sp around, 3 sc in last ch-2 sp, ch 3, sl st in last sc made, join in beg sc. Fasten off. ∎

Lacy Shells

DESIGN BY **MELISSA LEAPMAN**

SKILL LEVEL

BEGINNER

FINISHED SIZE

45 x 55 inches

MATERIALS

- Elmore-Pisgah Peaches & Crème medium (worsted) weight cotton yarn (2½ oz/122 yds/71g per skein): 20 skeins #42 tea rose
- Size H/8/5mm crochet hook or size needed to obtain gauge

4 MEDIUM

GAUGE

2 shells = 1¾ inches wide

PATTERN NOTES

Chain-3 at beginning of row or round counts as first double crochet unless otherwise stated.

Join with slip stitch as indicated unless otherwise stated.

SPECIAL STITCH

Shell: 4 dc in indicated place.

INSTRUCTIONS
AFGHAN

Row 1 (RS): Ch 207, sc in 2nd ch from hook, sc in next ch, *ch 1, sk next 4 chs, **shell** (see Special Stitch) in each of next 2 chs, ch 1, sk next 4 chs, sc in each of next 2 chs, rep from * across, turn.

Row 2 (WS): **Ch 3** (see Pattern Notes), dc in next sc, *ch 4, sk next 3 dc, sc in each of next 2 dc, ch 4, dc in each of next 2 sc, rep from * across, turn.

Row 3 (RS): Ch 1, sc in each of next 2 dc, *ch 1, shell in each of next 2 sc, ch 1, sc in each of next 2 dc, rep from * across, turn.

Next rows: Rep rows 2 and 3 alternately until piece measures approximately 55 inches, ending with row 3.

Last row: Ch 3, dc in next sc, *ch 3, sk next 3 dc, sc in each of next 2 dc, ch 3, dc in each of next 2 sc, rep from * across. Fasten off.

BORDER

Rnd 1 (RS): **Join** (see Pattern Notes) in upper right-hand corner, ch 1, [evenly sp 171 sc across to corner, 3 sc in corner, evenly sp 205 sc across to corner, 3 sc in corner st] around, join in beg sc.

Rnd 2: Ch 1, sc in first st, [ch 2, sk next sc, sc in next sc] around, with (sc, ch 2) twice in each center corner sc, join in beg sc.

Rnd 3: Sl st in ch-2 sp, ch 1, (sc, ch 3, sc) in each ch-2 sp around, join in beg sc. Fasten off. ■

Lavender Lace

DESIGN BY **ELIZABETH ANN WHITE**

SKILL LEVEL

INTERMEDIATE

FINISHED SIZE

42½ x 60 inches, excluding Fringe

MATERIALS

- Medium (worsted) weight yarn:
  40 oz/2,000 yds/1,134g lavender
- Size H/8/5mm crochet hook or size
  needed to obtain gauge

4 MEDIUM

GAUGE

7 dc = 2 inches; 4 pattern rows = 2½ inches

PATTERN NOTE

Chain-3 at beginning of row or round counts as
first double crochet unless otherwise stated.

INSTRUCTIONS
AFGHAN

Row 1: Ch 146, sc in 2nd ch from hook, sc in
next ch, ch 5, sk next 3 chs, [sc in each of next
3 chs, ch 5, sk next 3 chs] across to last 2 chs,
sc in each of last 2 chs, turn.

Row 2: Ch 1, sc in first st, sk next st, 5 dc in next
ch sp, [sc in center sc of next 3-sc group, 5 dc in
next ch sp] across to last 2 sts, sk next st, sc in
last st, turn.

Row 3: Ch 5, sk first dc, sc in each of next 3 dc,
ch 5, sk next dc, [sc in each of 3 center dc of
next 5-dc group, ch 5] across to last st, sc in last
st, turn.

Row 4: Ch 3 (see Pattern Note), 2 dc in first ch
sp, [sc in center sc of next 3-sc group, 5 dc in
next ch sp] across to last 3-sc group, sc in center
sc of last 3-sc group, 3 dc in last ch sp, turn.

Row 5: Ch 1, sc in each of first 2 sts, ch 5, [sc in
each of 3 center dc of next 5-dc group, ch 5]
across to last 2 sts, sc in each of last 2 sts, turn.

Rows 6–143: [Rep rows 2–5 consecutively] 34
times, ending last rep with row 3. At end of last
row, fasten off.

FRINGE

Cut 6 strands, each 14 inches long. Holding
all strands tog, fold in half, pull fold through
st, pull ends through fold, pull tight. Trim
ends evenly.

Attach Fringe in each ch sp across both short
ends of Afghan. ■

Mile-a-Minute Strip
Afghan

DESIGN BY **ELEANOR MILES-BRADLEY**

SKILL LEVEL

INTERMEDIATE

FINISHED SIZE
48 x 66 inches

MATERIALS
- Bernat Baby Coordinates light (light worsted) weight yarn (6 oz/ 431 yds/160g per ball):
  6 balls #01014 natural
- Size H/8/5mm crochet hook or size needed to obtain gauge
- Tapestry needle
- Fabri-Tac from Beacon Adhesives

GAUGE
7 dc = 2 inches; 2 dc rows = 1¼ inches

PATTERN NOTE
Join with slip stitch as indicated unless otherwise stated.

SPECIAL STITCHES
Decrease (dec): Yo, insert hook in next dc, yo, pull through, yo, pull through 2 lps on hook, sk next ch-1 sp, yo, insert hook in next dc, yo, pull through, yo, pull through 2 lps on hook, yo, pull through all lps on hook.

Picot: Ch 4, sl st in 4th ch from hook.

INSTRUCTIONS
AFGHAN
STRIP
MAKE 12.
Center: Ch 220, dc in 5th ch from hook, dc in each ch across, turn. *(217 dc)*

Rnd 1: Ch 4, dc in same st, *sk next 2 sts or next 2 chs, (dc, ch 1, dc) in next st or ch, rep from * 71 more times, (dc, ch 1, dc) 3 times around post of st at end of row* working in ch on opposite side of Center, (dc, ch 1, dc) in first ch, rep between * once, **join** *(see Pattern Note)* in 3rd ch of beg ch-4, **turn**.

Rnd 2: Sl st in next dc, ch 2, sk next ch-1 sp, dc in next dc *(dec)*, ch 2, [**dec** *(see Special Stitches)*, ch 2] around, join in beg dc, turn.

Rnd 3: Ch 1, sc in each dec around with (sc, **picot**—*see Special Stitches*, sc) in each ch sp around, join in beg sc. Fasten off.

Leaving 4 picots on each short end unworked, tack or glue 72 picots of 2 Strips tog. Rep with rem Strips. ∎

Purrfectly Pretty **Afghan**
DESIGN BY **JUDITH STOVER**

SKILL LEVEL
■□□ EASY

FINISHED SIZE
42 x 49 inches

MATERIALS
- Medium (worsted) weight yarn:
  28 oz/1,400 yds/794g off-white (MC)
  1 oz/50 yds/28g each 8 variegated or ombré colors and 8 solid colors (CC)
- Size G/6/4mm crochet hook or size needed to obtain gauge
- Tapestry needle

GAUGE
7 sc = 2 inches; 7 sc rows = 2 inches

PATTERN NOTES
Join with slip stitch as indicated unless otherwise stated.

Use a different contrasting color (CC) for each cat motif.

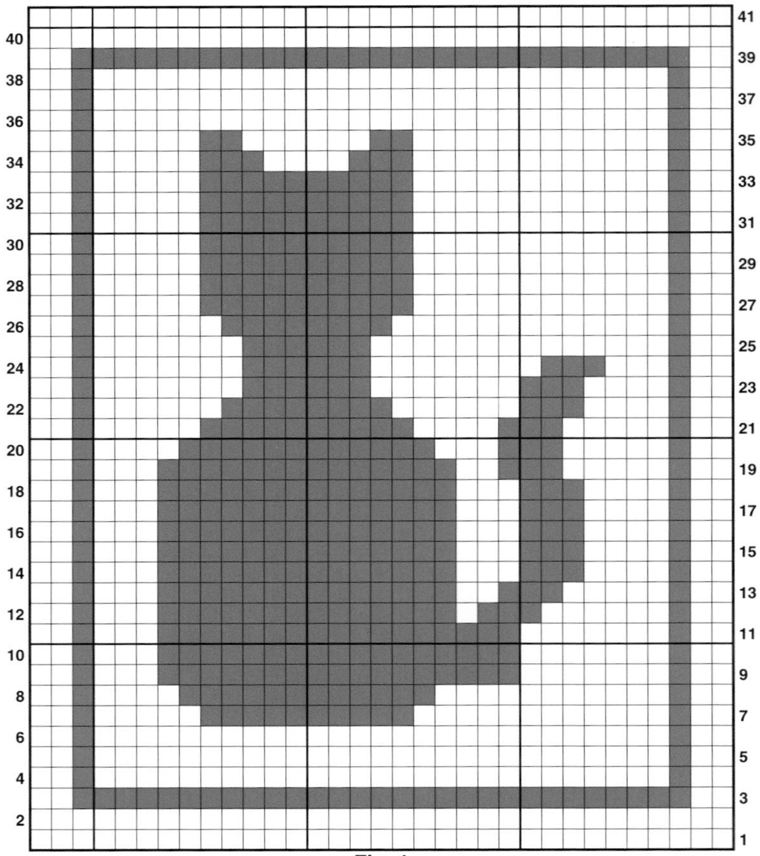

INSTRUCTIONS
AFGHAN
BLOCK
MAKE 16.
Row 1: With MC, ch 34, sc in 2nd ch from hook and in each ch across, turn. *(33 sc)*

Row 2: Ch 1, sc in each sc across, turn.

Rows 3–41: Ch 1, sc in each st across **changing colors** *(see Stitch Guide)* in last st according to **Chart** *(see Fig. 1)*, turn.

At end of row 41, fasten off.

Fig. 1
Purrfectly Pretty Afghan
Chart

COLOR KEY
□ MC
■ CC

ASSEMBLY
Holding RS tog, sew Blocks tog in 4 rows of 4 Blocks.

BORDER
Rnd 1: Join MC with sc in any sc, evenly sp sc around outer edge with 3 sc in each corner, **join** *(see Pattern Notes)* in beg sc.

Rnd 2: Ch 1, sc in each sc around with 3 sc in each center corner st, join in beg sc.

Rnd 3: Ch 1, sc in each of first 2 sts, ch 3, sk next st, [sc in each of next 2 sc, ch 3, sk next sc] around, join in beg sc. Fasten off.

FINISHING

With double strand of MC, tie bows at neckline of each cat, trim ends evenly. ■

Sapphire Shadows

DESIGN BY **JUNE SPIER BATEY**

SKILL LEVEL
■■■▢
INTERMEDIATE

FINISHED SIZE
42 x 73½ inches

MATERIALS
- Medium (worsted) weight yarn:
  18 oz/900 yds/510g each blue
  and gray
  7 oz/350 yds/198g white
- Size H/8/5mm crochet hook or
  size needed to obtain gauge

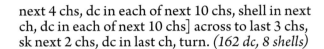

GAUGE
7 sc = 2 inches; 4 dc rows = 3 inches

PATTERN NOTES
Chain-3 at beginning of row or round counts as
first double crochet unless otherwise stated.

Join with slip stitch as indicated unless
otherwise stated.

SPECIAL STITCHES
Shell: (2 dc, ch 2, 2 dc) in place indicated.

Beginning large shell (beg lg shell): Ch 3,
(2 dc, ch 3, 3 dc) in place indicated.

Large shell (lg shell): (3 dc, ch 3, 3 dc)
in place indicated.

INSTRUCTIONS
AFGHAN
RIPPLE SECTION
MAKE 2.
Row 1: With gray, ch 204, dc in 6th ch from
hook, dc in each of next 9 chs, **shell** (see Special
Stitches) in next ch, dc in each of next 10 chs, [sk
next 4 chs, dc in each of next 10 chs, shell in next
ch, dc in each of next 10 chs] across to last 3 chs,
sk next 2 chs, dc in last ch, turn. (162 dc, 8 shells)

Row 2: Ch 3 (see Pattern Notes), sk next 2 sts,
dc in each of next 10 sts, shell in next ch sp, dc
in each of next 10 sts, [sk next 4 sts, dc in each
of next 10 sts, shell in next ch sp, dc in each of
next 10 sts] across to last 3 sts, sk next 2 sts, dc
in top of beg ch-5, turn.

Rows 3 & 4: Ch 3, sk next 2 sts, dc in each of
next 10 sts, shell in next ch sp, dc in each of
next 10 sts, [sk next 4 sts, dc in each of next 10
sts, shell in next ch sp, dc in each of next 10 sts]
across to last 3 sts, sk next 2 sts, dc in last st,
turn. Fasten off at end of last row.

Row 5: Join (see Pattern Notes) blue in first st, ch
3, sk next 2 sts, dc in each of next 10 sts, shell in
next ch sp, dc in each of next 10 sts, [sk next 4
sts, dc in each of next 10 sts, shell in next ch sp,
dc in each of next 10 sts] across to last 3 sts, sk
next 2 sts, dc in last st, turn.

Rows 6–8: Rep row 3.

Row 9: With gray, rep row 5.

Rows 10–36: [Rep rows 2–9 consecutively]
4 times, ending last rep with row 4.

GRAY MOTIF
MAKE 16.
Rnd 1: With gray, ch 4, 2 dc in 4th ch from hook,
ch 3, (3 dc, ch 3) 3 times in same ch, join in 3rd
ch of beg ch-3. (12 dc, 4 ch sps)

Rnd 2: Sl st in each of next 2 sts, sl st in next ch
sp, **beg lg shell** (see Special Stitches) in same ch
sp, **lg shell** (see Special Stitches) in each ch-3 sp
around, join in 3rd ch of beg ch-3. (4 lg shells)

Rnd 3: Sl st in each of next 2 sts, sl st in next ch sp, beg lg shell in same ch sp, 3 dc in sp between last lg shell and next lg shell, [lg shell in next ch sp, 3 dc in sp between last lg shell and next lg shell] around, join in 3rd ch of beg ch-3. Fasten off. *(4 lg shells, 4 dc groups)*

BLUE & WHITE MOTIF
MAKE 21.

Rnd 1: With blue, ch 4, 2 dc in 4th ch from hook, ch 3, (3 dc, ch 3) 3 times in same ch, join in 3rd ch of beg ch-3. Fasten off. *(12 dc, 4 ch sps)*

Rnd 2: Join white in first ch sp, beg lg shell in same ch sp, lg shell in each ch-3 sp around, join in 3rd ch of beg ch-3. Fasten off. *(4 lg shells)*

Rnd 3: Join gray in first ch sp, beg lg shell in same ch sp, 3 dc in sp between last lg shell and next lg shell, [lg shell in next ch sp, 3 dc in sp between last lg shell and next lg shell] around, join in 3rd ch of beg ch-3. Fasten off. *(4 lg shells, 4 3-dc groups)*

HALF MOTIF
MAKE 6.

Row 1: With blue, ch 4, (3 dc, ch 3, 4 dc) in 4th ch from hook, turn. Fasten off. *(8 dc, 1 ch sp)*

Row 2: Join white in first st, ch 3, 3 dc in sp between first 2 sts, lg shell in next ch sp, 4 dc in sp between last 2 sts, turn. Fasten off. *(8 dc, 1 lg shell)*

Row 3: Join gray in first st, ch 3, 3 dc in sp between first 2 sts, 3 dc in sp between 4th st and next lg shell, lg shell in next ch sp, 3 dc in sp between last lg shell and next st, 4 dc in sp between last 2 sts. Fasten off. *(14 dc, 1 lg shell)*

With gray, working through **back lps** *(see Stitch Guide)*, sew Motifs and Ripple Sections tog according to **Assembly Diagram** *(see Fig. 1)*. ∎

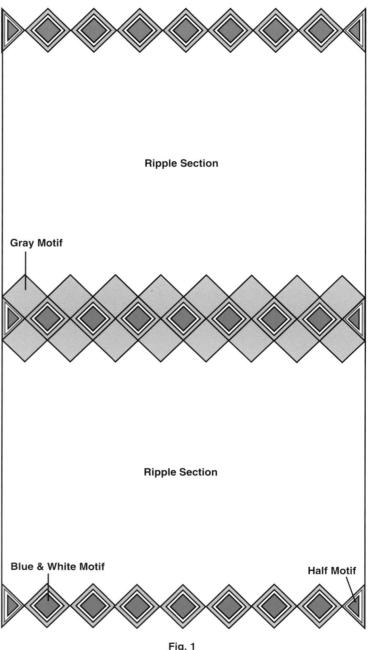

Fig. 1
Sapphire Shadows
Assembly Diagram

Seashells **Afghan**

DESIGN FROM **OLD-TIME CROCHET MADE EASY**

SKILL LEVEL

INTERMEDIATE

FINISHED SIZE
52 x 62 inches

MATERIALS
- Medium (worsted) weight yarn:
  42 oz/2,100 yds/1,191g dark gray
  21 oz/1,050 yds/595g each dark
  dusty rose and dusty rose
  14 oz/700 yds/397g coral
  11 oz/550 yds/312g peach
- Size H/8/5mm crochet hook
  or size needed to obtain gauge
- Tapestry needle

GAUGE
Motif = 8½ inches square

PATTERN NOTES
When a round begins with a double crochet, simply chain 3 for first double crochet.

Join with slip stitch as indicated unless otherwise stated

SPECIAL STITCH
Shell: Work 5 dc around vertical portion of indicated st.

INSTRUCTIONS
AFGHAN
SQUARE
MAKE 42.
Rnd 1: With dark gray, ch 4, sl st in first ch to form ring, ch 1, 8 sc in ring, **join** (see Pattern Notes) in beg sc, **turn.** (8 sc)

Rnd 2: Ch 1, 2 sc in first sc, [sc in next sc, 3 sc in next sc] 3 times, sc in next sc, sc in same sc as first 2 sc, join in beg sc, turn. (16 sc)

Rnd 3: Ch 1, 2 sc in first sc, [sc in each sc across to center sc of next corner, 3 sc in corner sc] around, ending with 1 sc in same sc as first 2 sc, join in beg sc, turn. (24 sc)

Rnd 4: Rep rnd 3, **do not turn.** Fasten off. (32 sc)

Rnd 5: Join peach in any center sc of any corner, ch 1, sc in same st, *sk next st, 3 dc in next st, sk next st, sc in next st, rep from * around, ending with sk last st, join in beg sc, do not turn. Fasten off.

Rnd 6: Join dark gray in center corner st, *(**dc**—see Pattern Notes, ch 1, tr, ch 1, dc) in center corner st, sc in top of center dc of next

3-dc group, 3 dc in next sc, sc in top of center dc of next 3-dc group, rep from * around, join in 3rd ch of beg ch-3, turn. Fasten off.

Rnd 7: Join peach in first dc of any corner, ch 1, sc in same dc, *ch 1, sc in next tr, ch 1, sc in next dc, **shell** (see Special Stitch) around vertical post of center dc of next 3-dc group of 2nd rnd down (peach row), sc in center dc of next 3-dc group of previous rnd, shell around vertical post of center dc of next 3-dc group of 2nd rnd down (peach row)**, sc in first dc of next corner, rep from * around, ending last rep at **, join in beg sc, turn. Fasten off.

Rnd 8: Working in sts on 2nd rnd down (dark gray), join coral in top corner tr inserting hook through center of sc previously worked in this st, ch 1, *sc in top of corner tr inserting hook through center of sc previously worked in this st, 3 dc under next ch-1 sp, sc in top of next dc, 3 dc in next sc, sc in top of center dc of next 3-dc group inserting hook through center of sc previously worked in this st, 3 dc in next sc, sc in top of next corner dc, 3 dc under next ch-1 sp, rep from * around, join in beg sc, **do not turn.** Fasten off.

Rnd 9: Join dark gray in center corner sc, (tr, ch 1, dc) in corner sc, *[sc in top of center dc of next 3-dc group, 3 dc in next sc] 3 times, sc in top of center dc of next 3-dc group, (dc, ch 1, tr, ch 1, dc) in next center corner sc, rep from * around, ending with (dc, ch 1) in same sc as first tr, join in beg tr, turn. Fasten off.

Rnd 10: With coral, rep rnd 7 with 1 more rep on each side of Square. (4 shells on each side)

Rnd 11: With dusty rose, rep rnd 8 with 6 groups of 3-dc on each side of Square.

Rnd 12: With dark gray, rep rnd 9.

Rnd 13: With dusty rose, rep rnd 7 with 6 shells on each side of Square.

Rnd 14: Working in sts of 2nd rnd down in dark gray row, join dark dusty rose in top of corner tr inserting hook in sc as before, work 3 dc in top of corner tr inserting hook in sc, *sc in top of next dc, **3 dc in next sc, sc in top of center

dc of next 3-dc group also inserting hook in sc, rep from ** 4 times, 3 dc in next sc, sc in top of next dc also inserting hook in sc, 3 dc in top of next tr, rep from * around, join in top of first dc, do not turn. Fasten off. (6 groups of 3-dc on each side, 1 group of 3-dc in each corner of Square)

Rnd 15: Join dark gray in center dc of any corner 3-dc group, ch 1, sc in top of center dc of 3-dc group, **ch 1, *3 dc in next sc, sc in top of center dc of next 3-dc group, rep from ** 5 times, 3 dc in next sc, ch 1, sc in top of center dc of next corner group, rep from * around, ending with ch 1, join in beg sc, turn. Fasten off.

Rnd 16: Join dark dusty rose around center corner dc of 3-dc group of 2nd rnd down (rnd 14), *shell around center dc of 3-dc corner group, ch 1, sc in top of center dc of next 3-dc group of rnd below (rnd 15), ** shell around post of 2nd rnd below, sc in top of center dc of next 3-dc group of rnd below, rep from ** 5 times, ch 1, rep from * 3 times, join in first dc, **do not turn.** Fasten off.

Rnd 17: This rnd is worked in sts of 2nd rnd down (dark gray rnd), also inserting hook through center sc sts previously worked on this rnd, join dark gray in center corner sc, work 2 dc in center corner sc, *1 sc under next ch-1 sp, **sc in each of next 3 dc, sc in next sc, rep from ** to next ch-1 sp, sc under next ch-1 sp, 3 dc in next corner sc, rep from * around, ending with dc in same sc as beg 2 dc, join in top of first dc, turn. (128 sts)

Rnd 18: Ch 1, 2 sc in same st as joining, *sc in each st to next center corner st, 3 sc in center corner st, rep from * around, ending with sc in same st as beg 2 sc, join in beg sc, turn.

Rnd 19: Rep rnd 18. Fasten off.

ASSEMBLY
Arrange Squares 6 x 7, and with dark gray from WS, matching sts and working in top lp only, sew Squares tog.

BORDER
Rnd 1 (WS): Join dusty rose in center corner sc, 3 dc in center corner sc, *sk next st, sc in next st, sk next st, 3 dc in next st, rep from * around,

using care to sp pattern so that there will be 3 dc in each corner of Afghan, join in top of beg dc, **do not turn**. Fasten off.

Rnd 2: Join dark gray in center corner dc, ch 1, sc in center corner dc, [3 dc in next sc, sc in top of center dc of next 3-dc group] around, join in beg sc, turn. Fasten off.

Rnd 3: Join dark dusty rose around center dc of corner of rnd 1, shell around center dc of corner of rnd 1, [sc in top of center dc of next 3-dc group of rnd 2 below, shell around post of center dc of next 3-dc group of rnd 1] around, join in top of first dc. Fasten off. ∎

Shells in the Round Afghan

DESIGN BY **DELLA BRENNEISE**

SKILL LEVEL

INTERMEDIATE

FINISHED SIZE
34 inches in diameter, excluding Fringe

MATERIALS
- Fine (sport) weight yarn:
  7 oz/630 yds/198g white
  2 oz/180 yds/57g blue
  1 oz/90 yds/28g pink
- Size H/8/5mm crochet hook or
  size needed to obtain gauge

2 FINE

GAUGE
6 shell rnds = 3 inches

PATTERN NOTES
Chain-3 at the beginning of row or round counts
as first double crochet unless otherwise stated.

Join with slip stitch as indicated unless
otherwise stated.

SPECIAL STITCHES
Beginning shell (beg shell): Ch 3 (dc, ch 2, 2 dc)
in place indicated.

Shell: (2 dc, ch 2, 2 dc) in place indicated.

INSTRUCTIONS
AFGHAN
Rnd 1: With white, ch 6, sl st in first ch to form
ring, ch 1, 16 sc in ring, **join** (see Pattern Notes)
in beg sc. (16 sc)

Rnd 2: [Ch 4, sk next sc, sc in next sc] 7 times,
ch 2, join with dc in joining sl st of last rnd.

Rnd 3: [Ch 4, sc in next ch sp] 7 times, ch 2, join
with dc in top of joining dc on last rnd.

Rnd 4: [Ch 5, sc in next ch sp] 7 times, ch 5,
sl st in top of joining dc on last rnd.

Rnd 5: Sl st in first ch-5 sp, **ch 3** (see Pattern
Notes), 5 dc in same ch-sp, 6 dc in each ch-sp
around, join in 3rd ch of beg ch-3.

Rnd 6: Ch 1, sc in first st, [ch 3, sk next dc, sc in
next dc] around, ch 1, join with hdc in beg sc.
(24 ch sps)

Rnd 7: [Ch 3, sc in next ch sp] around, ending with
ch 1, join with hdc in top of joining hdc of last rnd.

Rnd 8: [Ch 4, sc in next ch sp] around, ending
with ch 4, join in top of joining hdc of last rnd.

Rnd 9: Sl st in first ch-sp, **beg shell** (see Special
Stitches) in same ch sp, *ch 2, sc in next ch sp,
ch 2, **shell** (see Special Stitches) in next ch sp,
rep from * around, join in 3rd ch of beg ch-3.

Rnd 10: Sl st in next st and in first ch-2 sp, beg
shell in same ch sp, *ch 1, sc in ch-2 sp, ch 2,
sc in next ch-2 sp, ch 1**, shell in ch sp of next
shell, rep from * around, ending last rep at **,
join in 3rd ch of beg ch-3. Fasten off.

Rnd 11: Join pink in ch-2 sp of any shell, beg
shell in same ch sp, *shell in next ch-2 sp**,
shell in ch sp of next shell, rep from * around,
ending last rep at **, join in 3rd ch of beg ch-3.
Fasten off.

Rnd 12: Join white between any 2 shells, beg shell
in same sp, * sc in ch-2 sp of shell, shell between
next 2 shells, rep from * around, ending with sc
in top of shell, join in 3rd ch of beg ch-3.

Rnd 13: Sl st in next st and in first ch-2 sp of
shell, beg shell in same ch sp, sc in each sc and
shell in ch sp of each shell around, ending with
sc in last sc, join in 3rd ch of beg ch-3.

Rnd 14: Rep rnd 13. Fasten off.

Rnd 15: Join blue in any sc, ch 5, 5 dc in same st, *sc in ch-2 sp of next shell, 6 dc in next sc (*scallop*), rep from * around, ending with sc in ch-2 sp, join in beg sc. Fasten off.

Rnd 16: Join white in any sc between scallops, beg shell in same st, *sc in 3rd dc, ch 1, sc in 4th dc**, shell in next sc, rep from * around, ending last rep at **, join in 3rd ch of beg ch-3.

Rnd 17: Sl st in next st and in first ch-2 sp, beg shell in same ch sp, *shell in next ch-1 sp**, shell in next shell, rep from * around, ending last rep at **, join in 3rd ch of beg ch-3.

Rnd 18: Sl st in next st and in first ch-2 sp of first shell, sc in same ch sp, *ch 1, shell in ch sp of next shell, ch 1, sc in ch sp of next shell, rep from * around, join in beg sc.

Rnd 19: Sc in ch-1 sp, *ch 2, shell in ch sp of next shell**, [ch 2, sc in next ch-1 sp] twice, rep from * around, ending last rep at **, ch 2, sc in ch-1 sp, ch 2, join in beg sc. Fasten off.

Rnd 20: Join pink in ch-2 sp of any shell, beg shell in same ch sp, *sk ch-2 sp, shell in next ch-2 sp**, ch 2, shell in ch sp of next shell, rep from * around, ending last rep at **, join in 3rd ch of beg ch-3. Fasten off.

Rnd 21: Join white between any 2 shells, beg shell in same ch sp, *sc in ch-2 sp of next shell**, shell in sp between shells, rep from * around, ending last rep at **, join in 3rd ch of beg ch-3.

Rnds 22–26: Rep rnd 21. At end of last rnd, fasten off.

Rnd 27: Join blue in any sc, ch 3, 5 dc in same st, *sc in ch-2 sp of next shell, 6 dc in next sc, rep from * around, ending with sc in sc, join in beg sc. Fasten off.

Rnd 28: Join white in any sc, beg shell in same st, *sc in 3rd dc, ch 1, sc in next dc**, shell in sc between scallops, rep from * around, ending last rep at **, join in 3rd ch of beg ch-3.

Rnd 29: Sl st across and in first ch-2 sp, beg shell in same ch sp, *shell in ch-1 sp, shell in ch sp of next shell, rep from * around, ending with final shell, join in 3rd ch of beg ch-3.

Rnd 30: Sl st across and in first ch-2 sp, beg shell in same ch sp, *sc in ch-2 sp of next shell, shell in ch sp of next shell, rep from * around, ending with shell in ch-2 sp, join in 3rd ch of beg ch-3.

Rnd 31: Sl st across and in first ch-2 sp, beg shell in same ch sp, *ch 1, sc in next sc, ch 1**, shell in ch sp of next shell, rep from * around, ending last rep at **, join in 3rd ch of beg ch-3.

Rnd 32: Rep rnd 31.

Rnd 33: Sl st across and in first ch-2 sp, beg shell in same ch sp, *sc in ch-1 sp, ch 2, sc in ch-1 sp**, shell in ch sp of next shell, rep from * around, ending last rep at **, join in 3rd ch of beg ch-3. Fasten off.

Rnd 34: Join pink in ch-2 sp of any shell, beg shell in same ch sp, *shell in next ch-2 sp**, shell in ch sp of next shell, rep from * around, ending last rep at **, join in 3rd ch of beg ch-3. Fasten off.

Rnd 35: Join white between any 2 shells, ch 3, 2 dc in same sp, *sc in ch-2 sp of next shell**, 3 dc between next 2 shells, rep from * around, ending last rep at **, join in 3rd ch of beg ch-3.

Rnd 36: Sl st in next dc, ch 3, 2 dc in same st, *sc in next sc, sk next dc, 3 dc in next dc, rep from * around, join in 3rd ch of beg ch-3.

Rnd 37: Sl st in next dc, ch 3, 3 dc in same st, *sc in next sc, sk next dc, 4 dc in next dc, rep from * around, ending with sc in next sc, join in 3rd ch of beg ch-3.

Rnd 38: Sl st in next 2 dc, beg shell in same dc, *sc in next sc, sk next dc, 2 dc in next dc, ch 2, 2 dc in next dc, rep from * around, join in 3rd ch of beg ch-3. Fasten off.

FRINGE

Cut 4 strands blue, each 8 inches long. Fold strands in half, pull fold through st at bottom of Afghan, pull ends through fold, pull to secure.

Attach Fringe in each ch-2 sp on rnd 38. Trim ends evenly. ■

Star Dreamer

DESIGN BY **JOHANNA DZIKOWSKI**

SKILL LEVEL

INTERMEDIATE

FINISHED SIZE
72 inches across

MATERIALS
- Medium (worsted) weight yarn:
  21 oz/1,050 yds/595g black
  13 oz/650 yds/369g dark pink
  9 oz/450 yds/255g turquoise
- Size P/15/10mm crochet hook
  or size needed to obtain gauge

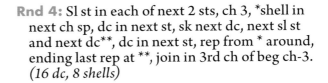

GAUGE
10 dc = 4 inches; 4 dc rows = 2½ inches

PATTERN NOTES
Chain-3 at beginning of row or round counts as first double crochet unless otherwise stated.

Join with slip stitch as indicated unless otherwise stated.

SPECIAL STITCHES
Shell: (2 dc, ch 2, 2 dc) in place indicated.

Picot: Ch 4, sl st in 4th ch from hook.

INSTRUCTIONS
AFGHAN
Rnd 1: With pink, ch 5, sl st in first ch to form ring, **ch 3** (*see Pattern Notes*), 15 dc in ring, **join** (*see Pattern Notes*) in 3rd ch of beg ch-3. (*16 dc*)

Rnd 2: Ch 1, sc in first st, ch 4, sk next st, [sc in next st, ch 4, sk next st] around, join in beg sc. (*8 sc, 8 ch-4 sps*)

Rnd 3: **Shell** (*see Special Stitches*) in next ch sp, [sl st in next st, shell in next ch sp] around, join in joining sl st on last rnd. (*8 sl sts, 8 shells*)

Rnd 4: Sl st in each of next 2 sts, ch 3, *shell in next ch sp, dc in next st, sk next dc, next sl st and next dc**, dc in next st, rep from * around, ending last rep at **, join in 3rd ch of beg ch-3. (*16 dc, 8 shells*)

Rnd 5: Sl st in next st, ch 3, dc in next st, *shell in next ch sp, dc in each of next 2 sts, sk next 2 sts**, dc in each of next 2 sts, rep from * around, ending last rep at **, join in 3rd ch of beg ch-3. (*32 dc, 8 shells*)

Rnd 6: Sl st in next st, ch 3, dc in each st across to next ch sp, *shell in next ch sp, dc in each st across to 2 sts at next indentation, sk next 2 sts**, dc in each st across to next ch sp, rep from * around, ending last rep at **, join in 3rd ch of beg ch-3. Fasten off.

Rnd 7: Join black in 2nd st, ch 3, dc in each st across to next ch sp, *shell in next ch sp, dc in each st across to 2 sts at next indentation, sk next 2 sts**, dc in each st across to next ch sp, rep from * around, ending last rep at **, join in 3rd ch of beg ch-3.

Rnds 8–12: Sl st in next st, ch 3, dc in each st across to next ch sp, *shell in next ch sp, dc in each st across to 2 sts at next indentation, sk next 2 sts**, dc in each st across to next ch sp, rep from * around, ending last rep at **, join in 3rd ch of beg ch-3. At end of last rnd, fasten off.

Rnd 13: With turquoise, rep rnd 7.

Rnds 14–16: Rep rnd 8. At end of last rnd, fasten off.

Rnd 17: Rep rnd 7.

Rnds 18–20: Rep rnd 8. At end of last rnd, fasten off.

Rnd 21: With pink, rep rnd 7.

Rnds 22–24: Rep rnd 8. At end of last rnd, fasten off.

Rnd 25: Rep rnd 7.

Rnds 26–28: Rep rnd 8. At end of last rnd, fasten off.

Rnd 29: With turquoise, rep rnd 7.

Rnds 30 & 31: Rep rnd 8. At end of last rnd, fasten off.

Rnd 32: Rep rnd 7.

Rnd 33: Rep rnd 6.

Rnd 34: With pink, rep rnd 7.

Rnd 35: Rep rnd 6.

Rnd 36: With black, sl st in next st, ch 2 (*counts as first hdc*), hdc in each st across to next ch sp, *(2 hdc, ch 2, 2 hdc) in next ch sp, hdc in each st across to 2 sts at next indentation, sk next 2 sts**, hdc in each st across to next ch sp, rep from * around, ending last rep at **, join in 2nd ch of beg ch-2.

Rnd 37: Sl st in next st, ch 1, sc in same st, sc in each st across to next ch sp, *3 sc in next ch sp, sc in each st across to 2 sts at next indentation, sk next 2 sts***, sc in each st across to next ch sp, rep from * around, ending last rep at **, join in beg sc. (*552 sc*)

Rnd 38: Ch 1, sc in each of first 5 sts, **picot** (*see Special Stitches*), *[sc in each of next 5 sts, picot] 12 times, sc in each of next 4 sts**, sc in each of next 5 sts, picot, rep from * around, ending last rep at **, join in beg sc. Fasten off. ∎

Southwest Ripple Afghan

DESIGN BY **ELEANOR MILES-BRADLEY**

SKILL LEVEL

■■■□
INTERMEDIATE

FINISHED SIZE
41½ x 56½ inches

MATERIALS
- Medium (worsted) weight yarn:
  18 oz/900 yds/510g medium brown
  7 oz/350 yds/198g each orange,
  tangerine, red, green and
  dark brown
- Size H/8/5mm crochet hook
  or size needed to obtain gauge

GAUGE
7 sc = 2 inches; 4 sc rows = 1 inch

SPECIAL STITCH
Long single crochet (lng sc): Working over
last row, insert hook in next st on row before
last, yo, pull lp through, yo, pull through 2 lps
on hook.

INSTRUCTIONS
AFGHAN
Row 1: With medium brown, ch 206, 2 sc in 2nd
ch from hook, sc in each of next 7 chs, sk next 2
chs, sc in each of next 7 chs, [3 sc in next ch, sc
in each of next 7 chs, sk next 2 chs, sc in each of
next 7 chs] across to last ch, 2 sc in last ch, turn.
(205 sc)

Rows 2–4: Ch 1, 2 sc in first st, sc in each of next
7 sts, sk next 2 sts, sc in each of next 7 sts, [3 sc
in next st, sc in each of next 7 sts, sk next 2 sts,
sc in next 7 sts] across to last st, 2 sc in last st,
turn. At end of last row, fasten off.

Row 5: Join orange with sc in first st, sc in same
st, *sc in next st, [**lng sc** *(see Special Stitch)* in

next st, sc in next st] 3 times, sk next 2 sts,
sc in next st, [lng sc in next st, sc in next st]
3 times**, 3 sc in next st, rep from * across,
ending last rep at **, 2 sc in last st, turn.

Row 6: Rep row 2. Fasten off.

Rows 7 & 8: With tangerine, rep rows 5 and 2.
At end of last row, fasten off.

Rows 9 & 10: With red, rep rows 5 and 2.
At end of last row, fasten off.

Rows 11 & 12: With green, rep rows 5 and 2.
At end of last row, fasten off.

Row 13: Join medium brown with sc in first st,
sc in same st, sc in each of next 7 sts, sk next 2
sts, sc in each of next 7 sts, [3 sc in next st, sc
in each of next 7 sts, sk next 2 sts, sc in each of
next 7 sts] across to last st, 2 sc in last st, turn.

Rows 14–16: Rep row 2. At end of last row,
fasten off.

Rows 17 & 18: With dark brown, rep rows 13
and 2. At end of last row, fasten off.

Row 19: Rep row 13.

Rows 20–22: Rep row 2. At end of last row,
fasten off.

Rows 23–142: [Rep rows 5–22 consecutively]
7 times, ending last rep with row 16.

EDGING
Row 1: Working across 1 straight edge, join
medium brown with sc in end of first row,
sc in end of each row across, turn.

Row 2: Ch 1, sc in each st across, turn.
Fasten off.

Rep on opposite straight edge.

BORDER

Rnd 1: Join dark brown with sc in end of row 2 on Edging before 1 short end, sc in same row, *sc in next row, work in established pattern across to Edging on next side, sc in end of next row, 2 sc in end of next row, working across long straight edge, sc in each st across*, working across next short end, 2 sc in end of first row, rep between * once, join with sl st in beg sc, **turn.**

Rnds 2 & 3: Ch 1, sc in each st around with 2 sc in each corner and working in established pattern across short ends of Afghan, join with sl st in beg sc, turn. At end of last rnd, fasten off. ■

Textured Aran Afghan

DESIGN BY **ANGELA TATE**

SKILL LEVEL

INTERMEDIATE

FINISHED SIZE
62 x 72 inches, excluding Fringe

MATERIALS
- Red Heart Super Saver medium (worsted) weight yarn (7 oz/ 364 yds/198g per skein): 10 skeins #313 Aran
- Size I/9/5.5mm crochet hook or size needed to obtain gauge
- Stitch markers

4 MEDIUM

GAUGE
13 dc = 5 inches; rnds 1–5 = 5 inches

PATTERN NOTES
Chain-3 at beginning of row or round counts as first double crochet unless otherwise stated.

Join with slip stitch as indicated unless otherwise stated

SPECIAL STITCH
Popcorn (pc): 5 dc in place indicated, drop lp from hook, insert hook in top of first dc of group, pull dropped lp through, ch 1 to secure.

INSTRUCTIONS
AFGHAN
FIRST STRIP
Rnd 1: Ch 178, 4 dc in 4th ch from hook (*first 3 chs count as first dc*), *dc in next ch, [**pc** (*see Special Stitch*) in next ch, dc in each of next 4 chs] 34 times, pc in next ch, dc in next ch*, 5 dc in last ch, working on opposite side of ch, rep between * once, **join** (*see Pattern Notes*) in 3rd ch of beg ch-3.

Rnd 2: Ch 3 (*see Pattern Notes*), dc in same st, 2 dc in each of next 4 sts, dc in each of next 173 sts, 2 dc in each of next 5 sts, dc in each dc around, join in 3rd ch of beg ch-3.

Rnd 3: Working in **front lps** (*see Stitch Guide*), working from left to right, ch 1, **reverse sc** (*see Fig. 1*) in each st around, join in beg reverse sc.

Rnd 4: Working in rem lps of rnd 2, ch 3, dc in same st as joining, 2 dc in each of next 9 sts, dc in each of next 173 sts, 2 dc in each of next 10 sts, dc in each st around, join in 3rd ch of beg ch-3.

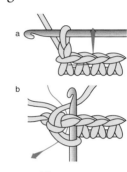
Fig. 1
Reverse Single Crochet

Rnd 5: Mark 6th and 103rd ch-5 sps with markers, ch 1, sc in first st, ch 5, sk next st, [sc in next st, ch 5, sk next st] around, join in beg sc. Fasten off. (*194 ch-5 sps*)

2ND–11TH STRIPS
Rnds 1–4: Rep rnds 1–4 of First Strip.

Marked ch-5 sps on First Strip will become center free sps on each end between Strips. Beg joining 2nd Strip in 4th ch-5 sp to the left of marker and leave 7 free ch-5 sps at each end of Strip as subsequent strips are joined.

JOINING RND
Rnd 5: Ch 1, sc in first st, [ch 5, sk next st, sc in next st] 9 times, [ch 2, sl st in 3rd ch of corresponding adjacent ch-5 sp on previous Strip, ch 2, sk next st on working Strip, sc in next st] 90 times, complete as for First Strip. Fasten off.

FRINGE
MAKE 22.
Cut 20 strands, each 12 inches long. Holding all strands tog, fold in half, pull fold through ch sp, pull ends through fold. Pull to tighten.

Attach Fringe in center ch-5 sp on each end of each Strip. Trim ends evenly. ■

Wavy Shells

DESIGN BY **MELISSA LEAPMAN**

SKILL LEVEL

BEGINNER

FINISHED SIZE
45 x 59 inches

MATERIALS
- Elmore-Pisgah Peaches & Crème medium (worsted) weight cotton yarn (2½ oz/122 yds/71g per skein):
  11 skeins #1 white
  10 skeins #19 peacock
- Size H/8/5mm crochet hook or size needed to obtain gauge

GAUGE
Shell = 1¼ inches wide

PATTERN NOTES
Chain-3 at beginning of row or round counts as first double crochet unless otherwise stated.

Join with slip stitch as indicated unless otherwise stated.

SPECIAL STITCH
Shell: (Dc, {ch 1, dc} 3 times) in place indicated.

INSTRUCTIONS
AFGHAN
Row 1 (RS): With peacock, ch 186, (dc, ch 1, dc) in 4th ch from hook (*first 3 chs count as first dc*), *sk next 3 chs, sc in each of next 7 chs, sk next 3 chs**, **shell** (*see Special Stitch*) in next ch, rep from * across, ending last rep at **, (dc, ch 1, 2 dc) in last ch, turn.

Row 2 (WS): Ch 1, sc in each st and each ch-1 sp across, ending with sc in last st, **change colors** (*see Stitch Guide*) to white in last st, turn.

Row 3: Ch 1, sc in first sc, working in **back lps** (*see Stitch Guide*) only, sc in each of next 3 sc, *sk next 3 sc, shell in next sc, sk next 3 sc**, working in back lps only, sc in each of next 7 sc rep from * across, ending last rep at **, working in back lps only, sc in each of next 3 sts, working through both lps, sc in last sc, turn.

Row 4: Ch 1, sc in each st and each ch-1 sp across, change to peacock in last st, turn.

Row 5: **Ch 3** (*see Pattern Notes*), (dc, ch 1, dc) in first sc, *sk next 3 sc, working in back lps only, sc in each of next 7 sc, sk next 3 sc**, shell in next sc, rep from * across, ending last rep at **, (dc, ch 1, 2 dc) in last sc, turn.

Next rows: Rep rows 2–5 consecutively until piece measures approximately 58 inches, ending with row 5.

Last row: Ch 1, sc in each of first 2 dc, sc in next ch-1 sp, sc in next dc, *hdc in each of next 7 sc**, [sc in next dc, sc in next ch-1 sp] 3 times, sc in next dc, rep from * across, ending last rep at **, sc in next dc, sc in next ch-1 sp, sc in each of last 2 dc. Fasten off.

BORDER
Rnd 1 (RS): Join white to upper right-hand corner, ch 1, [evenly sp 181 sc across to corner, 3 sc in corner st, evenly sp 219 sc across to corner, 3 sc in corner st] around, join in beg sc.

Rnd 2: Ch 4 (*counts as first dc and ch-1*), *sk next sc, dc in next sc, ch 1, rep from * around, with (dc, ch 1) 3 times in each center corner sc, join in 3rd ch of beg ch-4.

Rnd 3: Ch 1, sc in each dc and each ch-1 sp around, with 3 sc in each corner dc, join in beg sc.

Rnd 4: Ch 1, [sc in each of next 2 sc, ch 3, sl st in last sc] around, join in beg sc. Fasten off. ■

Pretty Popcorns Afghan

DESIGN BY **SUE CHILDRESS**

SKILL LEVEL

BEGINNER

FINISHED SIZE

38 x 43 inches

MATERIALS

- Fine (baby) weight yarn:
  21 oz/1,890 yds/595g pink
- Size F/5/3.75mm crochet hook or
  size needed to obtain gauge

2 FINE

GAUGE

5 sc = 1 inch; 5 sc rows = 1¼ inches

PATTERN NOTE

Join with slip stitch as indicated unless
otherwise stated.

SPECIAL STITCHES

Popcorn (pc): 5 sc in place indicated, drop lp
from hook, insert hook in first sc of group,
pull dropped lp through.

Shell: (2 dc, ch 2, 2 dc) in place indicated.

INSTRUCTIONS
AFGHAN

Row 1 (RS): Ch 164, sc in 2nd ch from hook
and in each ch across, turn. *(163 sc)*

Row 2: Ch 1, sc in each st across, turn.

Rows 3–12: Rep row 2.

Row 13 (RS): Ch 1, sc in each of first 11 sts, **pc**
(see Special Stitches) in next st, [sc in each of
next 19 sts, pc in next st] 7 times, sc in each of
last 11 sts, turn.

Row 14 (WS): Ch 1, sc in each st across, turn.
(163 sc)

Rows 15–62: Ch 1, work pattern across
according to **Chart** *(see Fig. 1 on page 68)*, sc in
each st across, turn.

Next rows: [Rep rows 13–62 consecutively]
twice.

Next rows: [Rep row 2] 5 times. At end of last
row, **do not turn**.

EDGING

Rnd 1 (RS): Ch 1, evenly sp sc around entire
outer edge, working 3 sc in each corner st, **join**
(see Pattern Note) in beg sc.

Rnd 2: Ch 3, (dc, ch 2, 2 dc) in same sc, [sk
next 3 sc, shell in next sc] around entire outer
edge, working at each corner (2 dc, {ch 2, 2 dc}
twice) in center sc of each corner, join 3rd ch of
beg ch-3.

Rnd 3: Sl st across to and in first ch-2 sp, ch 3, 4
dc in same ch-2 sp, [sc in sp between shells, 5 dc
in ch-2 sp of each shell] around, working at each
corner, 5 dc in first ch-2 sp, ch 1, 5 dc in 2nd ch-2
sp, join in 3rd ch of beg ch-3. Fasten off.

Wet to block Afghan. ■

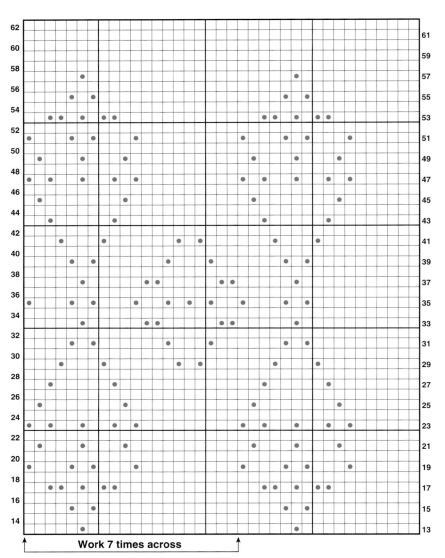

Work 7 times across

Fig. 1
Pretty Popcorns Afghan
Chart

STITCH KEY
☐ Sc
⊙ Pc

Lacy Delights

DESIGN BY **JOSIE RABIER**

SKILL LEVEL

EASY

FINISHED SIZE
33 x 51 inches

MATERIALS
- Aunt Lydia's Classic Crochet size 10 crochet cotton (1,000 yds per ball): 3 balls #201 white
- Size F/5/3.75mm crochet hook or size needed to obtain gauge
- Sewing needle
- Sewing thread
- Mauve ribbon roses with lace edge: 20
- 3/16-inch-wide avocado picot-edge ribbon: 2 yds

GAUGE
5 dc = 1 inch; 4 dc rows = 2 inches

PATTERN NOTES
Chain-3 at beginning of row counts as first double crochet unless otherwise stated.

Work with 2 strands of crochet cotton held together unless otherwise stated.

SPECIAL STITCH
Shell: (3 dc, ch 3, 3 dc) in place indicated.

INSTRUCTIONS
AFGHAN
Row 1 (RS): With **2 strands** held tog *(see Pattern Notes)*, ch 130, dc in 4th ch from hook *(first 3 chs count as first dc)*, dc in each of next 3 chs, *sk next 3 chs, dc in next ch, (ch 1, dc) 4 times in same ch, sk next 3 chs, dc in each of next 3 chs**, 3 dc in next ch, dc in each of next 3 chs, rep from * across, ending last rep at **, 2 dc in last ch, turn.

Row 2 (WS): Ch 3 *(see Pattern Notes)*, dc in same st, dc in each of next 3 dc, *sk next 2 dc, sc in next ch-1 sp, [ch 3, sk next dc, sc in next ch-1 sp] 3 times, sk next 2 dc, dc in each of next 3 dc**, 3 dc in next dc, dc in each of next 3 dc, rep from * across, ending last rep at **, 2 dc in last st, turn.

Row 3: Ch 3, dc in same st, dc in each of next 3 dc, *sk next ch-3 sp, dc in next ch-3 sp, (ch 1, dc) 4 times in same ch-3 sp, sk next ch-3 sp and next dc, dc in each of next 3 dc**, 3 dc in next dc, dc in each of next 3 dc, rep from * across, ending last rep at **, 2 dc in last st, turn.

Rows 4–63: [Rep rows 2 and 3 alternately] 30 times.

TOP BORDER

Row 64: Ch 1, sc in first st, ch 3, sk next 2 dc, sc in next dc, *ch 3, sk next 2 dc, sc in next dc, ch 3, sk next dc, sc in next dc, ch 3, sk next 2 dc, sc in next dc**, [ch 3, sk next dc, sc in next dc] 3 times, rep from * across, ending last rep at **, ch 3, sk next 2 dc, sc in last st, turn. (*53 ch-3 sps*)

Row 65: Ch 3, 2 dc in first ch-3 sp, 3 dc in next ch-3 sp, *shell (*see Special Stitch*) in next ch-3 sp, [3 dc in next ch-3 sp] twice, rep from * across, ending with 2 dc in last ch-3 sp, dc in last sc, turn. (*17 shells*)

Row 66: Ch 3, dc in next dc, sk next 2 dc, *dc in each of next 5 dc, (dc, ch 3, dc) in next ch-3 sp, dc in each of next 5 dc, sk next 2 dc, rep from * across, ending with dc in each of last 2 dc, turn.

Row 67: Ch 3, sk next 2 dc, *dc in each of next 5 dc, (dc, ch 3, dc) in next ch-3 sp, dc in each of next 5 dc, sk next 2 dc, rep from * across, ending with dc in last st, turn.

Row 68: Ch 3, sk next dc, *dc in each of next 5 dc, (dc, ch 3, dc) in next ch-3 sp, dc in each of next 5 dc**, sk next 2 dc, rep from * across, ending last rep at **, sk next dc, dc in last st, turn.

Rows 69–71: Rep row 68. At the end of last row, fasten off.

BOTTOM BORDER

Border foundation row (RS): Working in starting ch on opposite side of row 1, join 2 strands of white in base of first dc, ch 3, dc in same st, dc in each of next 3 chs, *sk next 3 chs, dc in next ch, (ch 1, dc) 4 times in same ch, sk next 3 chs, dc in each of next 3 chs**, 3 dc in next ch, dc in each of next 3 chs, rep from * across, ending last rep at **, 2 dc in last ch, turn.

Rows 1–8: Rep rows 64–71 of Top Border. At the end of last row, **do not fasten off**.

EDGING

With RS facing, working in ends of rows and in sts, ch 1, sc in end of last row, *[ch 3, sc in next